DRIVING BUY-IN

DRIVING BUY-IN

THE SCIENCE OF INFLUENCE WITH DATA

MICO YUK

WILEY

Copyright © 2026 by John Wiley & Sons, Inc. All rights reserved, including rights for text and data mining and training of artificial intelligence technologies or similar technologies.

Published by John Wiley & Sons, Inc., Hoboken, New Jersey.

No part of this publication may be reproduced, stored in a retrieval system, or transmitted in any form or by any means, electronic, mechanical, photocopying, recording, scanning, or otherwise, except as permitted under Section 107 or 108 of the 1976 United States Copyright Act, without either the prior written permission of the Publisher, or authorization through payment of the appropriate per-copy fee to the Copyright Clearance Center, Inc., 222 Rosewood Drive, Danvers, MA 01923, (978) 750-8400, fax (978) 750-4470, or on the web at www.copyright.com. Requests to the Publisher for permission should be addressed to the Permissions Department, John Wiley & Sons, Inc., 111 River Street, Hoboken, NJ 07030, (201) 748-6011, fax (201) 748-6008, or online at http://www.wiley.com/go/permission.

The manufacturer's authorized representative according to the EU General Product Safety Regulation is Wiley-VCH GmbH, Boschstr. 12, 69469 Weinheim, Germany, e-mail: Product_Safety@wiley.com.

Trademarks: Wiley and the Wiley logo are trademarks or registered trademarks of John Wiley & Sons, Inc. and/or its affiliates in the United States and other countries and may not be used without written permission. All other trademarks are the property of their respective owners. John Wiley & Sons, Inc. is not associated with any product or vendor mentioned in this book.

Limit of Liability/Disclaimer of Warranty: While the publisher and the author have used their best efforts in preparing this work, including a review of the content of the work, neither the publisher nor the author make any representations or warranties with respect to the accuracy or completeness of the contents of this work and specifically disclaim all warranties, including without limitation any implied warranties of merchantability or fitness for a particular purpose. No warranty may be created or extended by sales representatives, written sales materials or promotional statements for this work. The fact that an organization, website, or product is referred to in this work as a citation and/or potential source of further information does not mean that the publisher and author endorse the information or services the organization, website, or product may provide or recommendations it may make. This work is sold with the understanding that the publisher is not engaged in rendering professional services. The advice and strategies contained herein may not be suitable for your situation. You should consult with a specialist where appropriate. Further, readers should be aware that websites listed in this work may have changed or disappeared between when this work was written and when it is read. Neither the publisher nor author shall be liable for any loss of profit or any other commercial damages, including but not limited to special, incidental, consequential, or other damages.

For general information on our other products and services or for technical support, please contact our Customer Care Department within the United States at (800) 762-2974, outside the United States at (317) 572-3993 or fax (317) 572-4002. For product technical support, you can find answers to frequently asked questions or reach us via live chat at https://support.wiley.com.

If you believe you've found a mistake in this book, please bring it to our attention by emailing our reader support team at wileysupport@wiley.com with the subject line "Possible Book Errata Submission."

Wiley also publishes its books in a variety of electronic formats. Some content that appears in print may not be available in electronic formats. For more information about Wiley products, visit our web site at www.wiley.com.

Library of Congress Control Number: 2026932122

ISBN 9781394307494 (Hardback)
ISBN 9781394307500 (ePub)
ISBN 9781394307517 (ePDF)

Cover Design: Wiley
Cover Image: © Modon/stock.adobe.com

To God, my lovely mother Nadina, my sisters Soo and Anna Maria, my mentors, customers, students, and podcast fans—none of this would've happened without you.

CONTENTS AT A GLANCE

INTRODUCTION — XV

CHAPTER 1
THE $777-BILLION BREAKDOWN — 1

CHAPTER 2
THE DISCOVERIES THAT CHANGED EVERYTHING — 13

CHAPTER 3
THE DATA STORYTELLING (4D) FRAMEWORK™ — 27

CHAPTER 4
THE THREE SIGNS OF INFLUENCE — 45

CHAPTER 5
DISCOVER—ASK THE RIGHT QUESTIONS — 63

CHAPTER 6
DEFINE—STORIES THAT STICK — 85

CHAPTER 7
DESIGN—VISUALS THAT DRIVE ACTION — 113

CONTENTS AT A GLANCE

CHAPTER 8
DELIVER—PRESENT TO WIN BUY-IN   143

CHAPTER 9
MASTERY—THE 90-DAY PATH   167

CHAPTER 10
THE MOVEMENT   185

    ACKNOWLEDGMENTS   203

    ABOUT THE AUTHOR   207

    INDEX   209

CONTENTS

INTRODUCTION	XV
CHAPTER 1	
THE $777-BILLION BREAKDOWN	1
The Decision Acceleration Crisis	2
The People Problem	4
The Two Things We Can Actually Influence	7
Decisions Are Emotional	9
CHAPTER 2	
THE DISCOVERIES THAT CHANGED EVERYTHING	13
Discovery #1: Our Brains Are Wired For Stories	16
Discovery #2: You Can Measure Buy-In	20
Sign #1: Clarity (the Nod)	22
Sign #2: Buy-In (the Questions)	23
Sign #3: Action (Timeline Thinking)	23
The Buy-In Method	24
CHAPTER 3	
THE DATA STORYTELLING (4D) FRAMEWORK™	27
Pillar 1: Story	30
The Three Villains That Kill Buy-In	31
The Push-And-Hope Trap	33

CONTENTS

Your Role: The Guide, Not The Hero	34
The Data Storytelling (4D) Framework	36
Step 1 → Discover: Ask the Right Questions	38
Step 2 → Define: Create Stories That Stick	39
Step 3 → Design: Create Visuals That Drive Action	41
Step 4 → Deliver: Present to Win	42
The Missing Piece	43

CHAPTER 4
THE THREE SIGNS OF INFLUENCE — 45

Pillar 2: Signals	47
The People Problem	48
We're Measuring The Wrong Thing	51
The Three Signals	53
Sign #1: Clarity—The Nod Test	54
Sign #2: Buy-In—The Questions Test	55
Sign #3: Action—The Timeline Test	57
The Sequence Matters	59
Decision Drivers	60

CHAPTER 5
DISCOVER—ASK THE RIGHT QUESTIONS — 63

Why Your Questions Are Failing You	66
Step 1: Discover—You Need Context First	67
Three Discovery Questions That Reveal Readiness	69
Question 1—*Who* do you picture using this?	69
Question 2—*When* do you see this being needed?	71
Question 3—*What* is the story behind this?	72
The Three Discovery Questions In Action	74
Why These Questions Work	75
When The Questions Don't Work	80
Your Unfair Advantage	83

CHAPTER 6
DEFINE—STORIES THAT STICK — 85

- The Real Alignment Crisis: False Consensus — 88
- The Art Of Storyboarding — 90
- Step 2: Define—Building The Story — 91
- The Three Storyboard Sprints — 93
  - Sprint 1: Align the Vision (60–90 Minutes) — 93
    - The Setup — 95
    - The Rules of Engagement — 95
    - How to Run the Sprint — 96
    - By the End of Sprint 1 — 100
  - Sprint 2: Validate the Plan (24–48 Hours) — 100
    - What to Watch For — 101
    - The Process — 101
    - The Validation Checklist — 102
    - The Updated Storyboard — 103
    - The Mindset — 103
  - Sprint 3: Commit to Action (60 Minutes) — 104
    - Walking Back into the Room — 104
    - When the Data Disagrees — 105
    - The Walkthrough — 105
    - Lock In the Commitment — 106
    - What You Leave With — 107
- Why The Storyboard Works — 108
- When To Use The Storyboard (And When To Skip It) — 109

CHAPTER 7
DESIGN—VISUALS THAT DRIVE ACTION — 113

- Why Most Dashboards Die — 115
- The Anatomy Of A Decision Tile — 116
- Step 3: Design Visuals That Drive Action — 118

CONTENTS

THE 4-TILE STRUCTURE	119
Row 1: The Goal Banner	120
Row 2: Three Decision Tiles	121
The One-Screen Rule	124
From Storyboard to Slide Deck	125
Why This Works	127
When Design Goes Wrong	132
Your Turn	134
Step 1: Build The Goal Banner	135
Step 2: Build the First Decision Tile	136
Step 3: Build The Second and Third Decision Tiles	137
Step 4: Test It	138
Ready To Deliver	139

CHAPTER 8
DELIVER—PRESENT TO WIN BUY-IN

	143
Death By A Thousand Touchpoints	145
Talk *To* People, Not *At* Them	147
Step 4: Present To Win Buy-In	149
The Opening: Win Trust in 60 Seconds	150
Step 1: Start with a Short Greeting, Then State Their Need (10 seconds)	151
Step 2: Show Why It Matters (20 seconds)	152
Step 3: Set Expectations (30 seconds)	152
The Delivery Formula: Stay in Human Mode	153
Step 1: Say the Content	154
Step 2: Pause	154
Step 3: Ask Yourself a Question about Them	155
Step 4: Watch for the Three Signs of Influence	155
Step 5: Adjust Based on What You See	155
The Closing: Provide Clear Next Steps	156
A Quick Reference To The Formula	159
Why It Works	159

CONTENTS

When You Lose The Room 162
Try This Monday 163
You Made It! 164

CHAPTER 9
MASTERY—THE 90-DAY PATH 167
John: The Wrong Problem 167
Nadina: The Everyone Problem 171
Cabria: Reading The Room 175
The 90-Day Truth 177
Your 90-Day System 178
    Weeks 1–4: Discovery 178
    Weeks 5–8: Storyboarding 179
    Weeks 9–12: Three Signs of Influence 180
Four Pitfalls 180
The Transformation 181
From Mastery To Movement 183

CHAPTER 10
THE MOVEMENT 185
What Actually Changes 187
It Starts With One 188
Your Edge In The AI Age 192
The Buy-In Method Manifesto 193
    The Oath 195
The Vision 196
Your Move 198

ACKNOWLEDGMENTS 203

ABOUT THE AUTHOR 207

INDEX 209

INTRODUCTION

You know the feeling. You just finished presenting. The room is quiet. Someone says, "Thanks, this is really helpful." And you walk out with absolutely no idea if anything you said will matter.

This is called winging it.

Ninety-nine percent of professionals who present data do it. I would know. I was one of them.

For years, I spent endless nights perfecting my models—checking my analysis, building dashboards. Then I'd walk into the room, present my findings... and hope something stuck.

Sometimes I would get a dry "Yes, this looks great," or "Thank you, this helps," but most of the time I was left wondering, would anyone actually use my work?

Wasted hours. Endless revisions. And that ongoing, nagging feeling that no one truly valued what I did.

Sound familiar?

I'll never forget the VP who thanked me for my "comprehensive analysis," then turned around and made the exact opposite decision two days later. I sat in my car in the parking lot, staring at the nothing for 20 minutes. That's when I knew something had to change.

INTRODUCTION

If you've ever left a meeting wondering whether you got buy-in—if anyone is actually going to do anything with your data—this book is for you.

WHAT I DISCOVERED

It took me years of getting my butt handed to me before I figured out what I'm about to share with you.

I tried everything the industry told me to try: better visualizations, cleaner slides, executive summaries, books on communication, storytelling, even public speaking.

I kept improving the things everyone said to improve. And I kept walking out of meetings with no clue whether anything I said would lead to action.

Then something clicked.

The problem wasn't my data. It wasn't my dashboards. It wasn't my presentation skills.

The problem was that I had no idea what was happening in the room. I couldn't tell if people were actually buying in or just being polite.

I couldn't read the signals that would tell me whether my work was about to drive a decision or die in someone's inbox.

Once I learned to see those signals—once I understood the patterns—everything shifted.

I stopped hoping my presentations would work and started knowing when they were working. I could see buy-in forming in real time. I could adjust mid-conversation when things went sideways. I could predict who would take action and who was just nodding to be nice.

And here's what surprised me most: none of it required me to become a different person. I didn't need to develop some magical charisma I wasn't born with. It was systematic. It was learnable. And it works whether you're

INTRODUCTION

an introvert, an extrovert, or someone who'd rather hide behind a spreadsheet than speak to a room.

WHAT THIS BOOK WILL TEACH YOU

This book gives you the two things that transformed my career and the careers of more than 20,000 professionals I've trained:

- **Data Storytelling Framework:** A four-step structure—Discover, Define, Design, Deliver—that turns any analysis into decision fuel. It's not about making prettier charts. It's about structuring your message the way the brain actually processes information—so people stop overthinking and start acting.
- **The Three Signs of Influence:** A method for measuring buy-in in real time. You'll learn to spot three specific behaviors that tell you—with surprising accuracy—whether someone is moving toward a decision or just being polite. Once you see the signs, you can't unsee them.

Here's what that looks like in practice.

- **Before this book:** You walk into a meeting with a data dump and a wish. You present your analysis, get a polite "thanks," and spend the next week wondering if anything will happen.
- **After this book:** You walk into that same meeting with a story structured to drive a decision—not just display data. You read the room in real time. You adjust when you're losing them. And you walk out knowing exactly who's going to act—and who was just being polite. You'll know the difference between a nod that means "I get it" and one that means "please stop talking."

INTRODUCTION

From order-taker to decision driver.

I've watched professionals make that shift—from invisible analyst to the person leadership calls first.

Not because they got louder.

Because they got systematic.

WHO THIS BOOK IS FOR

This book is for anyone who presents data to influence decisions:

If you're an **analyst** who's tired of watching your recommendations collect dust while leadership goes with their gut—I've been there. I spent years building the analysis nobody used.

If you're a **manager** who walks out of every presentation with no idea whether people actually heard you or were just waiting for it to end—I know that silence. I've lived in it.

If you're a **consultant** who can see the answer but can't get the client to move—I've watched my best insights die in a PDF no one opened.

And if you're an **executive**, a **project manager**, a **marketing lead**—anyone who's ever needed a room to stop nodding and start acting—this book was built in those rooms.

If you present data and need people to do something with it, you're in the right place.

WHY THIS MATTERS NOW

Here's the thing: as AI generates insights faster than ever, the bottleneck isn't analysis anymore—it's human decision-making.

The technical skills that used to set you apart? AI is catching up. Fast. Routine analysis that took weeks now takes minutes. The dashboards you spent months building? AI can build them in a fraction of the time.

The professionals who thrive in the next decade won't be the ones with the best models or the cleanest dashboards. They'll be the ones who can influence humans to act on those insights.

This isn't about soft skills. It's about survival skills. The ability to measure engagement, create buy-in, and drive decisions—these are the capabilities that AI can't replicate. These are the skills that make you irreplaceable.

Every meeting you walk into without this is a meeting where gut feelings win and your data loses.

While 99% of data professionals keep wondering if their work matters, you'll know exactly how to make it count. While others push information and cross their fingers hoping something sticks, you'll create buy-in and watch decisions happen.

This isn't about fearing AI. This is about collaborating with AI and knowing when your AI-generated insights are actually influencing decisions.

This isn't about learning storytelling. This is about mastering the behavioral science of human influence.

THE INVITATION

I believe every professional who presents data deserves to know when their work matters. Not wonder. Not hope. Know.

I believe the era of "push and hope"—where we present our best work and just hope someone acts on it—is a career death sentence in the age of AI.

INTRODUCTION

And I believe you picked up this book because you're done guessing.

This book is called *Driving Buy-In* because that's exactly what you'll learn to do—not hope for it, not beg for it, but systematically drive it using the behavioral science of influence.

You're not just learning a methodology. You're joining a movement of professionals who refuse to wing it anymore. From data presenters to decision drivers. No more order-taking. No more hoping. No more wishing.

The push-and-hope era of our career is officially over.

This is the end of dead insights.

Let's get to work.

CHAPTER ONE
THE $777-BILLION BREAKDOWN

"A wealth of information creates a poverty of attention."
—Herbert A. Simon

I remember it like yesterday. I was in a boardroom in New York presenting a dashboard. We'd spent three months working on it. Late nights. Early mornings. Weekends sacrificed. The data was solid. The insights were golden. The recommendations would save the company millions.

So when the VP leaned back in his chair and said, "I'm not seeing what you're saying here," I absolutely panicked.

He wasn't asking for clarification. He wasn't confused about a metric. He simply wasn't buying it. I knew it was game over when he picked up his phone and started scrolling.

I'm not going to lie. I left that boardroom feeling completely deflated. I went back to my hotel room and honestly cried—not because I felt incompetent, but because I could not seem to explain my work well enough for my client to get it. All those hours. All that effort. And my analysis was DOA (dead on arrival).

It hurt. But it also pushed me to discover something much bigger, something that would change my career and thousands of others.

Because what I didn't know then was this: The moment wasn't about data. It wasn't about me. It wasn't even about the client.

I had just experienced the $777-billion crisis quietly destroying our industry, and no one was talking about it.

THE DECISION ACCELERATION CRISIS

Most professionals who present data have lived a moment like that—where months of analysis are DOA due to a few seconds of confusion, which leads to a lack of interest and ends with a "gut decision." Unfortunately, that New York "report review" session wasn't an isolated incident. It was a preview of a much larger issue happening everywhere.

Organizations have tripled spending on data talent. Data tool budgets are hitting record highs. Data consulting is through the roof. Companies are building massive analytics platforms, hiring armies of data scientists, investing billions in AI and machine learning.

And yet?

Decision speed, acting on insights, and user adoption are at an all-time low. The math ain't mathing.

Organizations have spent $777 billion on data talent over the past five years. Even more on software and consulting. And yet? Eighty percent of insights never influence a single decision. We're spending more money generating unused insights than most countries' GDPs. Make it make sense.

We are constantly being asked to "accelerate decisions," yet we're given tools that aren't designed for that purpose—not bad tools, just wrong tools.

The Wrong Tools

- Faster queries. Prettier dashboards.
- Chart libraries. Visualization training.
- Analytics platforms. AI-powered insights.
- Data pipelines. Computing power.

All great tools. But here's what nobody is teaching us.

The Missing Skills

- How to get stakeholders to trust you.
- How to tell if someone's ready to make a decision.
- How to read the room during meetings.
- How to influence people without being pushy.

And guess what? No one is rushing to fix it. Why? There's zero incentive.

- Vendors make money selling software licenses, not faster decisions.
- Research firms get paid to identify problems, not solve them.
- Management consultants get paid by the hour, not by the results.
- Training companies sell courses on technical skills, not people skills.

Meanwhile, we—the data stewards, who actually have to present the data—get stuck holding the bag. We get handed these tools and told to "accelerate decisions."

So what do we do? We bury our heads in the sand, build great-looking dashboards and reports, and track user adoption to CYA (cover your butt), knowing fully well that they will have zero impact on decision speed.

If we really want to be data-driven, let's stop measuring logins and actually look at the data. For every dollar spent generating faster insights, decision-making actually slows down. The math still ain't mathing, and the industry keeps ignoring it.

That's why I wrote this book.

I wrote it because I desperately needed it myself ten years ago, when I went from being an abstract artist and performing with my flute to becoming a data scientist—a data scientist in a creative body, that is. When I first entered the data industry and got my a** handed to me, I almost quit.

But then I uncovered the real problem.

While technical tools and training were everywhere, no one was teaching the one thing that I was being asked to do: Get people to take action on my insights.

This insights-to-decision breakdown isn't a technical problem—it's a human problem. The "people problem" everyone whispers about during lunch breaks and in private DMs isn't just another culture issue. It's something much deeper.

Our entire industry has been pouring money into the wrong buckets for decades. We've been throwing technology at human problems—and wondering why nothing changes.

But here's the truth no leader wants to say out loud. Admitting they've been investing in the wrong things for years is career suicide. So they keep buying tools and funding technical training because it's "tangible" and easier to justify.

Meanwhile, the real problem keeps growing.

THE PEOPLE PROBLEM

Here's what baffles me. We spend four years in college learning statistics and coding. Python and SQL. Linear regression and recommendation engines. Forecasting algorithms that would make NASA jealous.

But nobody teaches us "How to Survive Getting Ambushed in Meetings 101" or "How to Get People to Actually Use Your Work."

But the moment a leader leans back in their chair and says, "I'm not seeing what you're trying to say here," we go complete blank, impostor syndrome kicks in, and we find ourselves rushing to justify our data.

We're like the emperor with no clothes—technically brilliant but socially blind.

Welcome to what's happening in conference rooms and online meetings all across the world, all day, every day.

The results?

- In lunchrooms: "Did you see how he completely ignored my recommendations?"
- During cubicle drive-bys: "I stayed up all night working on that report, and they still went with their gut."
- In private Slack DMs: "I'm so tired of these ad hoc report requests. I feel like an order-taker.

Sound familiar?

But when we discuss it as a team, we say: "Yeah, it's a cultural problem." Code word for "Until leadership changes, learn to live with it."

After ten years and working with thousands of users, it's time to push back.

If it's such a culture problem, why can't HR fix it? They've tried everything—leadership coaching, presentation workshops, team-building retreats.

None of it has worked, and the data clearly shows it.

Here's why: HR teaches people to communicate better, not how to measure if their communication is actually working. They haul you off to presentation workshops to learn how to design better slides and reports instead of learning to design for how the human brain processes information and makes actual decisions.

And while HR is focused on making us better presenters, we have another problem brewing: our leadership is obsessed with measuring the wrong metrics! Data teams track login rates without knowing if the users actually understood the action they need to take. They measure dashboard clicks while the real decisions are being made by the gut. Even worse, slide decks have zero measurement—just present and pray something sticks.

And it's not just organizations that are suffering—it comes at a high personal career cost, too. Constant justification. Crippling impostor syndrome. Performance reviews dinging you for "communication skills" while your work gets ignored.

The willful delusion that self-service, AI, or more technical training will fix these problems is just that—a delusion. The truth is most of us who handle and present data were never equipped with the people skills or emotional intelligence (EQ) to drive decisions. I would know. I was one of them.

So what does "we have a people problem" actually mean? That humans are broken and need fixing? Of course not. We can't change how the human brain makes decisions. It's how we're wired. It's neuroscience, not a bug.

Instead, we need to learn to work with it—to admit that the problem isn't them; it's the system that didn't train us correctly. We're showing up to a gunfight with butter knives (in my Clint Eastwood voice).

We've been trained to solve human problems with technical solutions. We present good information, hoping something sticks, then wonder why people still go with their gut. The push-and-hope method seldom works.

Here's the thing: while we can't control how the human brain makes decisions or processes information, there are two specific things we can influence that change everything. Thankfully, neither of them requires us to get a PhD in human behavior or an MBA in psychology.

THE TWO THINGS WE CAN ACTUALLY INFLUENCE

While you're reading this book, another business professional is about to be blindsided. They spent three weeks building a nice dashboard, report, or slide deck with clear data-driven actions and a perfect analysis. They went in to present it to their stakeholders, only to hear, "Thanks for the hard work. We're actually just going to stick with what we did last year." Translation: "Thanks for the good insight, but we're going with our gut."

This isn't happening once in a while; it's actually the norm. No matter how perfect the analysis, how well designed the data visualization, decision-makers use their gut to make important decisions, even when the data says otherwise.

Here's what drives me nuts! There's a huge push for being data-driven, yet 90% of leaders admit to still going with their gut. The data they should be using to drive these decisions—88% of it—is sitting unused in dashboards and reports no one trusts or uses.

I don't know if it's sheer ignorance or just our way of avoiding the truth, but as I stated earlier, we dig our heads in the sand and start measuring things that we have no control over:

- Daily logins for reports and dashboards
- Time spent on analytics platforms
- Number of Excel exports created

Let me ask you a question: Can you force someone to log in? Can you control how long they spend looking at your dashboard? Can you prevent them from exporting to Excel? Can you force them to pay attention to your slides?

Of course not. So why are these considered to be success metrics?

None of these metrics have any impact on decision-making. Zero. Zilch. More logins don't drive action. Longer time on the platform doesn't drive decisions. Exporting to Excel is a clear sign of analysis paralysis—or not enough information. And with slide decks, you get zero measurement at all.

You and I know these are vanity metrics, and they serve more to cover our a** than anything else. Someone can spend 30 minutes on your dashboard and still ignore every recommendation. They can also stare at your slide deck and be sleeping with their eyes open.

The data industry is broken. We don't accelerate decisions—we slow them down. We build solutions, ship them, and don't have to ensure they actually work as long as we have "something to show." Hence why we have millions of reports and dashboards created every year with a user adoption rate averaging 25%—and that number hasn't moved in a decade.

Other industries that also invest billions, like Hollywood movie studios, don't just put out a movie, hope for the best, and then count box office receipts. Before the movie comes out, they carefully run test screenings to measure audience reactions in real time, looking at which scenes viewers zone out and reach for their phones. They reshoot those scenes before the wide release to ensure audiences are glued to their seats.

In data, we get excited if someone spends more than 30 minutes on our analytics platforms. Forget that studies show users spend 1.8 hours daily searching for information just to do their jobs. That's $1.7 million lost annually per 100 employees. That means there's a high chance they're in search mode, not action-taking mode. Make it make sense.

So what should we actually be measuring?

Simple. Two metrics:

1. How you influence stakeholders to increase the likelihood that they will actually take action
2. Whether or not your influence is actually working

These two metrics determine whether you are seen as a trusted advisor who helps to accelerate decisions or as someone who remains an order taker tackling never-ending ad hoc requests. In the age of AI automation, this isn't just about getting promoted—it's about staying relevant and providing value.

But you can't influence anyone until you understand how decisions actually get made. Spoiler alert: it's not by having better data.

DECISIONS ARE EMOTIONAL

You know what amazes me? God designed the human brain in fascinating ways, and we, as humans, are still trying to figure out how it works. Thankfully, in the 1990's, a neuroscientist named Antonio Damasio discovered something pretty amazing about the human brain. While studying a man named Elliot, who had just undergone brain surgery to remove a brain tumor, he realized that he had damaged the side of his brain that processes emotions.

Elliot could still think logically, remember things, even get dressed and go to work like a normal person, but Damasio discovered he had one major issue: he couldn't make a single decision—not even a simple one like "what shirt to wear" or "what to eat for lunch." He could analyze like everyone else, but his brain could never get to a decision.

Damasio concluded something that our industry has gotten terribly wrong: *humans make decisions with emotions and then use logic to justify them*—not the other way around.

> **WHAT THE GUT IS REALLY ASKING**
>
> Before any decision, the gut runs this checklist:
>
> **1.** Am I safe? (survival)
> **2.** Do I belong? (connection)
> **3.** Will this help me succeed? (status)
>
> If your solution doesn't address at least one of these, people don't care.

They use their heart (emotions) first and their mind (logic) second.

So while you've been busy creating neat spreadsheets and getting your data perfectly indexed, there is an 88% chance it will only trigger analysis paralysis and never lead to a single decision.

Decisions are made before any data is ever seen.

Decisions are emotional, not logical.

That's why most presentations and dashboards are DOA (dead on arrival)—and why most slide decks feel like DBP (death by PowerPoint).

The reason you get a polite nod and a quiet "Thank you for the hard work" after your presentation, and then nothing happens, isn't random. It's scientifically predictable. It's happening because we're doing exactly what we've been trained to do: get in, get to the point, stick to the facts, address any questions, and hope they make a decision.

Most of the time we lose them mentally before we even get started. Here's what they experience and why they go often with their gut:

- **We talk to the wrong side of the brain:** We talk to the analytical part of their brain, while the gut makes all the decisions. It's like trying to turn on the TV with the garage door remote.
- **We deliver information overload:** We show everything we think they'll need to see to make an "educated decision" on the screen. The reality? We broke their brain. It's like going on a first date and dumping your entire life story when asked, "Tell me about yourself."
- **We put people on the defense:** We waltz in saying, "Here's what the analysis shows..." They hear, "Everything you're doing is wrong." Of course they get defensive. Who wants to be told they're wrong?

The fact is, most of the "best practices" we've been taught about data when it comes to driving decisions are designed to fail. We've been taught to fight against the way the brain works to process information and make decisions. Then we wonder why we keep losing to the gut. Why decision-making keeps slowing down instead of speeding up?

Write this on a sticky note like I did and keep it on your desk:

> *People decide with their gut (emotions) and then use your data to justify what they've already decided—not the other way around.*

That's why giving people more data creates analysis paralysis, not action.

That's why the push-and-hope mentality drove me nuts for years—it was all I knew. Damasio's findings changed everything.

My thesis: If decisions follow predictable emotional patterns, then we should be able to influence and measure decision readiness, right?

There's a saying, "If you can't measure it, you can't manage it."

Everything changed when I asked myself two questions: How do we create decision readiness before presenting data? Can we measure it as it happens?

In Chapter Two, I reveal the two amazing discoveries that took me and thousands of our students from "hoping our users would take action" to "predictably increasing the likelihood that they would take action." The push-and-hope era of your career is officially over.

CHAPTER TWO

THE DISCOVERIES THAT CHANGED EVERYTHING

"If you can't measure it, you can't manage it."
—Peter Drucker

A few months ago, a senior analyst from a large life sciences company stayed back after our workshop. She waited until everyone left, then turned to me. "Mico, can I be honest?" she said quietly. "Half the time I leave a meeting thinking, 'Okay, that went well,' and then nothing happens. No progress. Just follow-up and delays. And I'm really starting to wonder if maybe the problem is me. Is there something I'm not seeing?"

Let me translate this for you: what she was really asking was, How do I know when I actually have true buy-in?

I've been there. Here's the reality: you don't become a senior analyst if you can't get stakeholders to act on your recommendations.

The problem?

We can't control how long it takes someone to make a decision or take action.

Sometimes you present your analysis and recommendations, and in one meeting, voila! Everyone gets it. Everyone's on board. Everyone is ready to act. Other times? Same quality work. Same stakeholders. Same presentation approach. Yet you're stuck in three follow-up meetings and a never-ending "reply all" email thread. . . while your recommendations gather dust.

So what is the difference in these two experiences? The people? The timing? The data?

As a data scientist turned analyst turned leader, I spent years trying to figure this out. I was convinced I had no control. If they bought in, great. If not, back to the drawing board for another round.

Then I discovered something that changed everything. I had way more control than I thought—just not over the things I'd been focused on.

I couldn't control their personalities, their politics, or their competing priorities. But I could control two things that mattered far more: how I structured my communication and what to watch for in my stakeholders' reactions.

That's when I stumbled onto something that changed my career—not one discovery, but two.

If you're a business or data professional who presents numbers to drive decisions—dashboards, decks, or reports—these two discoveries will change the way you work.

- **Discovery #1—Story:** The first thing I learned is that the human brain is wired for stories, not data. If we want folks to buy in to our

ideas and recommendations and take action, we have to tell stories with our data.
- **Discovery #2—Signals:** The second thing I learned is that stakeholder buy-in can be measured. It follows three predictable behavioral signals you can see happening in real time. If we want to influence outcomes, we have to learn to recognize these patterns.

I know what you're thinking: *Stories and signals, Mico? That sounds like soft skills—the stuff they teach the sales folks.* Ten years ago, I'd have agreed with you. But trust me when I tell you, it's the survival skill that no one told us we needed—the difference between being an order-taker and a decision driver. This isn't about becoming a people person or becoming more charismatic. It's not even soft skills. It's behavioral science—measurable, repeatable, and backed by decades of research on how humans make decisions. Across neuroscience, behavioral research, and elite training programs—from business schools to Navy SEALs—the same pattern exists: decisions follow an emotional arc you can see, measure, and guide.

And let's be real: whether you like it or not, we're all in sales. Whether you're trying to sell an idea, a recommendation, a budget increase, or the next game-changing initiative, you're still selling. It's a huge paradigm shift, and one I pushed back on for years as the data person who believed "data should speak for itself." Turns out, there is a way to influence stakeholders and get them to take action on your data.

It starts with seeing a few simple patterns. Once you see them, you can't unsee them. Suddenly, those impossible stakeholder meetings start turning into final decisions. Your follow-ups get shorter, the back-and-forth decreases, and decisions are being made.

The first discovery came from the most unexpected place—a keynote that almost didn't happen.

DISCOVERY #1: OUR BRAINS ARE WIRED FOR STORIES

I was staring at my KPI (key performance indicator) Blueprint spreadsheet—30 columns, 15 rows, and 450 cells of data. Powerful, but ugly.

But it worked. No more metric chaos. No more overwhelm.

The KPI Blueprint was dead simple: plug in your metric and then fill out the details on the right. Department. Use case. Short Name. Definition. Formula. Chart Views. Drill down. Format. Owner. Source. Viewing period. Updating period. Alerts. Security. Status. Then, boom. You are left with clearly defined metrics with clear owners.

The challenge? Convincing an audience of data and business professionals to actually use it. To trust the process. To fill it in, cell by cell, and watch metric overload become a thing of the past.

As I stood backstage, talking to myself, I could see thousands of heads in the audience waiting for my keynote. "How in the world am I going to do this?" I thought to myself. "I can't just go column by column. They'll fall asleep—or worse—some may walk out."

I had two minutes to decide: do I bore them with a column-by-column walkthrough, or do I tell them the absurd, hilarious stories of what actually happens when you try to get stakeholders to fill this thing out?

I went with the stories.

Metric definition? "Oh, I want to track customer satisfaction." Great. Define it. "Uh... you know... like... how satisfied are they?" This is where things get interesting. The metric definition should simply describe—in layman's terms—what the metric actually is. No jargon. Just the human version of the metric. And this is when you find out real fast that many stakeholders don't actually know what they're asking for. They have an emotional sense of the metric, but not a logical definition. I warned the audience: if you define it, you own it. Watch them backpedal.

Metric formula? Oh, this one is even worse. Not only do stakeholders have no idea what they're asking for, they usually have no clue how to measure it. Ask for a formula? Crickets. If the number is wrong (and it usually is), guess who gets blamed? So I told the audience: never give them the formula first. Always let them tell you how to calculate it. Their logic, their math. It protects you and ensures the calculation is correct.

Metric owner? More crickets. Adding metrics to the dashboard? Everyone's hand shoots up. Owning the metric? Different story. It's like musical chairs—whoever is left standing when the music stops is stuck with it. Nobody wants to be accountable. No owner, no validation.

And it went on like that. Data in the system that turned out to be a spreadsheet on someone's laptop, security fields no one could explain, alerts nobody wanted to own. Every column had a story—and every story proved the same point: The KPI Blueprint works because it forces users to validate and own their metrics instead of just depending on the data team.

As I walked through the anecdotes of each column, something unexpected happened. People started nodding, laughing, raising their hands, and taking notes. Not only did that keynote go on to take me all over the world, but the KPI Blueprint was downloaded over 10,000 times.

And then came the crazy part—the invitations to speak.

Google, Meta, and Harvard—all because I ditched the boring column walkthrough and told the story they didn't even know they needed.

To be honest, I was so young and introverted. Who knows what would have happened if that keynote had failed? I really wanted to help folks like me, and I knew I had a great tool they could use.

I didn't think of it as a breakthrough moment back then, but I did become obsessed with understanding why it worked. Why did telling the story of each column trigger 10,000 downloads?

So I started digging into neuroscience.

Here's what I discovered: human brains are wired for stories, not spreadsheets.

If you want to get buy-in, drive action, and have people take action on your data, you have to learn to tell compelling stories. It's not a nice-to-have.

But here's what nobody tells you: data storytelling is powerful. It works—but not by itself.

After that keynote, I doubled down. I studied storytelling. I practiced it. I implemented everywhere—dashboards, reports, discovery sessions, meetings. And it worked. My presentations improved. Engagement surged. People nodded more, laughed more, and engaged more. I got invited to speak at companies I'd only dreamed of.

But then came the brutal revelation: engagement isn't adoption.

Even with all the momentum, our actual user adoption wasn't changing. Dashboards were still not being used beyond the initial hype. We had no idea if anyone would take action on our data. When we checked? Some did. Some didn't. There was no way to predict or guarantee it.

After a few years of teaching data storytelling, one thing became clear. Stories definitely got attention, but they didn't always create buy-in—the emotional investment people need before they take action.

Engagement without emotional investment is entertainment. We're in this to drive action, to drive decisions.

I needed a way to measure the difference, to know when stakeholders were bought in and ready to act. Not just nodding politely, but emotionally invested.

Turns out, someone had already cracked this code—just not in the data world. You know who figured this out decades ago? NBA superstar Magic Johnson.

In the late 1990s, Magic was not just playing basketball. He was upgrading the urban communities where he grew up in South Central L.A. After opening movie theaters, he wanted to upgrade the experience by offering Starbucks to moviegoers.

He flew to Seattle determined to pitch Howard Schultz (founder of Starbucks and then CEO). Armed with the best analysts, charts, and projections, the opportunity was clear.

Schultz wasn't buying it. He had never allowed anyone to open a Starbucks, and Magic's projections weren't about to change that.

But Magic didn't give up. He invited Schultz to L.A. It was a Friday night screening of *Waiting to Exhale*, starring Whitney Houston, at one of his busiest theaters. As the lights dimmed, almost 500 women filled every seat. Schultz and Johnson snuck in the back and watched as the audience leaned into every scene. The crowd laughed, whispered, and kept returning to the concession stand.

In that moment, Schultz saw what no spreadsheet could ever show: people craving connection. He saw community. And he was sold.

Starbucks went on to open 125 Community Stores in urban neighborhoods. They didn't just meet their financial projections—they crushed them. They outperformed expectations, sparking local pride, lifting foot traffic, and forging brand loyalty that data alone had never predicted. Magic sold his stake in 2010 for $100 million and became part of the ownership group that purchased the L.A. Dodgers for $2.2 billion. Today, they're worth over $7 billion.

Magic didn't change the numbers. He changed how Schultz felt about the numbers. By letting Schultz feel the energy of the crowd, Magic tapped into the emotions that data alone could never reach.

Charts don't change minds. Emotions do.

That's when I realized there had to be a science to this—not just intuition, not charisma, a repeatable structure behind why some stories move people and others fall flat.

This became the foundation of what many came to know as my Data Storytelling Framework, or the 4Ds for short: discover, define, design, and deliver.

The 4Ds mirror the way humans naturally move from curiosity to clarity to meaning to action. It's the same cognitive path your stakeholders follow every time they decide whether to care, agree, or act.

Chapter 3 will show you exactly how to use it, whether you're building a dashboard, creating a report, or designing a slide deck.

DISCOVERY #2: YOU CAN MEASURE BUY-IN

When I left New York, I took a federal gig at Joint Base Anacostia–Bolling in Washington, D.C. I thought things would be different.

I was wrong.

What took two months in corporate took six–nine months in the federal government. My requirements-gathering sessions became the definition of insanity:

- **Session 1:** Gather requirements.
- **Session 2:** "Actually, we need something different."
- **Session 3:** Update everything.
- **Session 4:** "Wait, that's not what we want."
- **Session 5:** Start over.

Six and a half years of engineering school. A year of PhD statistics classes. And I'd gone from data scientist to professional babysitter.

I loved working with data. With humans? Not so much. Not because they were bad or anything—I just couldn't seem to get them to collectively buy in to anything: the insights, the recommendations, nothing.

Then one night, while at dinner in downtown Washington, D.C., my buddy Derek—a former Navy SEAL—pulled me aside while I was venting about another "revisit" session.

"Mico, you need to relax. Slow down a bit, and read the room. Once you do that, you will have better control over the conversation. You're in reactive mode."

I looked at him, frustrated. "What do you mean?" That was rich coming from Derek. He's the one who recruited me for this gig.

He got up to take a quick smoke outside but turned back. "It's the classic people problem. You're a smart girl. You'll figure it out. Wheels up at 6 a.m."

His words echoed in my head: "Read the room. Control the conversation. The classic people problem."

Navy SEALs go through years of psychological conditioning, mental imagery training, reading situations under pressure, and battle-proofing their minds. If Derek said I needed to "read the room," I knew there was something to it.

Over the next few months, Derek became my drill sergeant. Every car ride to and from the base, he would replay my meetings, pointing out what I missed, what I could've done differently, and what to try next time.

"Tech projects always nail the processes and technology, but they drop the ball when it comes to the actual people they need to serve," Derek explained.

He was right. I had frameworks for everything. Methodologies. Tools. Best practices.

But a framework for reading people? I didn't even know that existed.

"As a Navy SEAL, reading people isn't a nice-to-have skill—it's life or death. I have to know in real time if someone's truly on board or just going through the motions. You're building analytics that could help troops on the ground, and you can't tell if any of your stakeholders are actually going to use what you're giving them? You're guessing whether critical intel is going to sit in a dashboard or actually reach the people who need it? That's insane."

And he was right.

From that day forward, I felt like Neo in *The Matrix*. I had taken the red pill. There was no going back. I became obsessed again. I watched everything: faces, body language, questions, energy shifts. I couldn't shut it off.

Slowly but surely, my sessions started to change.

Instead of getting ambushed, I could see pushback coming and address it before it happened. I could see when someone was genuinely interested or just being polite, just by the questions they asked.

For the first time in my career, I wasn't walking into meetings hoping something would "stick." I was walking in knowing what to look for and how to pivot.

As an introvert, this felt like a hidden superpower!

I spent years developing and silently testing what I was seeing—which nods meant understanding versus just following along, which questions signaled buy-in versus curiosity, what signals meant they were really ready to act.

Without realizing it, I'd discovered the *Three Signs of Influence*.

Not another communication technique, but an actual, measurable way to track influence in real time.

Here's how it works:

Sign #1: Clarity (the Nod)

When people truly understand you, their brains literally change. You can see it when they nod.

Research by Petty and Briñol at Ohio State University has shown this. There's a massive difference between "I'm listening" nods and "I get it" nods. Polite nods are faster and more robotic—their minds are elsewhere. "I get it" nods are slower and more deliberate, as they process what you're saying.

Sign #2: Buy-In (the Questions)

The pronouns people use in their questions reveal everything.

Harvard researcher Karen Huang's work has shown this. When people shift from "you/your" to "we/our" language, they're psychologically bought in.

When someone asks "What's *your* approach here?" they're still evaluating your ideas.

When they ask "What's *our* approach here?" they've mentally joined your team and are bought into the idea.

The shift is subconscious. They can't fake it.

Sign #3: Action (Timeline Thinking)

When people mention timelines, they're ready to act.

Gollwitzer's research on implementation intentions showed this. When people use timeline language, they've mentally shifted from consideration to execution.

"If we do this" versus "When we do this" are completely different. The shift from "if" to "when" means the decision is already made.

Here's the critical part: each sign builds on the previous one. You can't skip steps.

Someone asking implementation questions before they really understand your concept will crash and burn during execution.

Someone who understands and asks we/us questions but never mentions timelines? They're not ready to commit.

> **KEY INSIGHT: THE THREE SIGNS OF INFLUENCE**
>
> **1.** CLARITY — Slow nods (they get it)
> **2.** BUY-IN — "We/our" language (they own it)
> **3.** ACTION — Timeline talk (they're ready)

Miss one, back to the drawing board. Buy-in isn't just a feeling. It's measurable. A game-changer for anyone presenting data.

THE BUY-IN METHOD

What I just shared with you isn't two separate discoveries—it's the method that transformed my career and the careers of over 20,000 data and business professionals across the world.

It's the method I wish someone handed me on day one of my data analytics career. It would literally have saved me years of rework, follow-up meetings, delays, and the dreaded "let's revisit this next quarter."

And it has a name: the Buy-in Method.

> **KEY INSIGHT: THE BUY-IN METHOD**
>
> **1.** Pillar 1: STORY — Structure your message (Data Storytelling (4D) Framework)
> **2.** Pillar 2: SIGNALS — Measure your influence (Three Signs of Influence)

The Three Signs of Influence—clarity, buy-in, and action—show you exactly where your stakeholders are and what they need next to move forward.

The second pillar gives you the power to read the room and guide decisions with confidence.

When you bring these two pillars together, something amazing happens—you don't just become a data storyteller; you become a decision driver.

Decision drivers don't present data.

They don't just make slides look prettier.

They don't just communicate better.

They guide decisions.

They walk into a room knowing:

- How to tell the story behind the data, and
- How to read the behavior behind the reactions.

They can clearly see when their audience is confused by looking at their faces.

They can see when buy-in is wavering by the questions being asked.

They can see when their stakeholders are ready to take action.

Once you master the two pillars of the Buy-in Method, you stop pushing and hoping something will stick . . . and you start knowing with confidence it did.

You stop waiting for action, and start driving it.

That is the promise of using the Buy-in Method.

For leaders, the Buy-in Method turns every analyst, PM, and manager into a decision driver—so your initiatives stop being stalled and start moving forward in days versus quarters.

In the next chapter, I'm going to show you exactly how to use it.

First, I'll break down the Data Storytelling (4D) Framework so you can build stories that cut through the noise and create clarity.

Then, I'll unpack the Three Signs of Influence so you can measure buy-in in real time.

Finally, I'll show you how to apply it to the systems you use every day: dashboards, reports, QBRs, stakeholder meetings, and strategic conversations.

By the end of this book, you won't just tell better data stories. You'll know in real time if your stakeholders are actually bought in and ready to act.

You'll drive decisions with confidence.

CHAPTER THREE

THE DATA STORYTELLING (4D) FRAMEWORK™

"The universe is made of stories, not of atoms."
—Muriel Rukeyser

Ten minutes before his weekly leadership meeting, the CEO pulled me aside.

"Reporting can wait," he said quietly. "We need to fix something else first."

That's how I found myself walking into a glass-walled conference room in San Francisco with three frustrated executives, almost no context, and absolutely no room for error.

Sunlight spilled across the long wooden table, reflecting off the projector. I could feel the tension in the room.

Three strong personalities. One $10 million problem that was growing more expensive by the day.

The company was growing fast, but their reporting systems were outdated—ignored analytics, unused reports, an exhausted team drowning in ad hoc requests. My team had been brought in by the CIO to help them modernize their analytics and build a platform that could support their growth—but that would have to wait.

There was no warm-up. No political background. No time to build trust. I took a deep breath. Honestly, if there was ever a time I needed our framework to work, it was right now.

I introduced myself quickly, sketched the storyboard on the whiteboard, and handed each leader a marker and a set of colored sticky notes. "Do you mind writing your answers down instead of discussing them out loud?" I asked. "We'll walk through everything after. I just want your full thoughts first." They nodded.

Then I asked my first question: "If we solve this problem in the next 90 days, what does success look like?" They wrote in silence.

When they were done, John went first. His voice cracked. "I wrote about avoiding layoffs, but honestly. . ." He paused, looking down. "Ten years ago, we faced a similar situation. I had to let 40 people go. I don't want to do that again."

I froze, marker still in hand. This wasn't about frameworks anymore. The COO's shoulders dropped. The VP of Sales uncrossed her arms.

I could feel the energy shift and the air get lighter.

Dan, the COO, read next: "I'll read what I wrote, but I actually agree with John." The VP of Sales, nodded: "Same here."

I looked at each of them: "So does everyone agree that avoiding layoffs is our definition of success?" Three nods. I let out a quiet sigh of relief. One question shifted everything.

They weren't fighting about the losses in Texas. They'd been fighting about different definitions of success. And the moment layoffs entered the conversation, every agenda turned into a single, shared priority.

From there, the story almost wrote itself. A few department-specific metrics surfaced, but once we got to the heart of the problem, the noise faded away.

Within 90 minutes we had:

- A clear Goal
- Agreed-upon Key Metrics
- A handful of Insights and Actions I could validate with the data

That day in California proved something I've suspected but never seen unfold so quickly: the right question doesn't just gather requirements. It unlocks the real reason alignment had been blocked in the first place.

Story and emotion—not more data—were the real leverage in the room.

I didn't need data. I didn't need a fancy slide deck. I needed the right questions.

> Dashboards don't drive action. Stories do.

What you just witnessed wasn't a fluke. Three executives. Three competing agendas. Ten minutes later, they were aligned and emotionally connected—not because I'm some storytelling genius, but because I let the structure do the heavy lifting.

That's the part most people miss. Influence isn't magic. It's method.

It wasn't my luck or intuition. I applied the same framework I've used in boardrooms, Zoom calls, and million-dollar planning sessions. A framework anyone can learn.

That's the power of the Data Storytelling (4D) Framework in action—the first part of the Buy-In Method you're about to learn.

PILLAR 1: STORY

California proved something critical: when you don't have a good structure, you walk into meetings hoping they "get it." Crossing your fingers. Hoping something sticks.

> Hope is not a strategy. Structure is.

That's the difference between those who drive decisions and 88% whose insights get ignored.

Pillar 1 of the Buy-In Method™ gives you that structure.

The Story. A clear, repeatable framework that turns your analysis into a decision map—one that people can follow, remember, and act on.

But here's the thing nobody told us: story alone isn't enough. You also need to be able to see whether your story is actually working.

This is where Pillar 2 (Signals) comes in (Figure 3.1).

Your real-time feedback system. Story tells you what you build. Signals tell you whether it's working.

When you use them together? Meetings get lighter. Decisions happen faster. You stop explaining and start guiding. You walk out knowing—not hoping—that someone will take action on your data.

But there are three villains that threaten to destroy your influence before you even walk into the room.

Figure 3.1 The Buy-In Method—two pillars working together

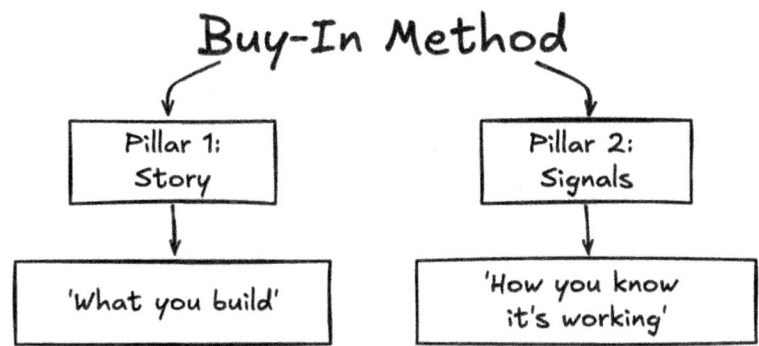

THE THREE VILLAINS THAT KILL BUY-IN

Every analytics project starts with good intentions. Yet, most fail.

Not because of the data. Not because of you.

They fail because you're fighting three hidden forces that threaten to kill your influence before you even walk into the room.

1. **The Gut:** Decisions are made with emotion, not data.

    I've watched managers nod along in agreement for 15 minutes—until the data suggests cutting their pet project. All of a sudden, their tone changes.

    "What assumptions are you using here?"

    Most leaders don't even realize they're making emotion-driven decisions. Pressure, fear, ego, urgency. The Gut quietly takes over and steers interpretation, priority, and action unless you surface and structure it.

When the Gut starts running the meeting, data doesn't stand a chance.

> When clarity drops, emotions take over.

2. **The Gap:** When stakeholders don't know what they need, we get treated like order takers.

   Vague requests. Technology-focused solutions. Half-formed questions.

   This isn't incompetence. It's uncertainty. It's shame. Leaders are ashamed to admit they're lost, so they throw random requests, hoping to find something that sticks.

   I've sat through hundreds of kickoff meetings where an exec says "just show me what the data says" as a crutch. They're not being difficult—they're being human.

   When the Gap shows up, alignment goes out the window!

3. **The Myth:** Letting data speak is a fantasy.

   Data doesn't drive decisions. Stories do.

   Without structure and narrative, even the cleanest analysis is DOA (dead on arrival).

   This one fooled me for years. I believed that if I just made the dashboard cleaner, clearer, prettier—people would get it.

   Wrong. They didn't. They never do.

   Good data alone is never enough.

   The Myth convinces smart people that data will do all the work. It never does.

These three villains may be invisible, but their impact is not. They've killed more data projects than bad data ever could.

I've lived through all three. I've watched The Gut kill projects I spent months building. I've played order-taker when executives treated me like an analytics vending machine. And I've made hundreds of reports that nobody touched. For years, I thought the answer was better data. It wasn't.

Most of us don't even know we're fighting them. We just keep revising our reports, updating the dashboard, redesigning our slides hoping things will change.

They will not.

Not unless you understand what you're up against.

That's what the Data Storytelling (4D) Framework helps you do.

THE PUSH-AND-HOPE TRAP

But here's the trap. Even when we spot these villains, most of us have no idea what to do next. So, we default to what we know.

The Push-and-Hope method. Push it out and hope something sticks. Onto the next project.

This was me at the start of my data science career. I was moving so fast I didn't really have time to care whether anyone actually used my analysis. I'd present my findings, answer a few questions, send the deck, and jump straight to the next fire drill.

Then at year-end review, I'd get dinged on communication. "Great data scientist, but hard to understand sometimes."

What did that even mean? And I wasn't alone.

Every data scientist and analyst I knew was on the Push-and-Hope treadmill. It went something like this.

Collect the data. Analyze the data. Dig up the insights. Screenshot the dashboard. Paste it into slides. Add a few recommendations. Throw in more data for "context." Deliver it... and hope they get it.

We all thought this was normal. We thought this was the job.

But no one told me I had to influence stakeholders. No one told me that to act on my data was part of my responsibility.

> Clarity doesn't drive action. Buy-in does.

I thought my job ended when they understood the analysis. It doesn't. Push-and-Hope ends at clarity. Driving decisions requires readiness.

Nobody taught us that clarity is step one. That our job doesn't end when they nod—it ends when they are ready to move.

So we stop there. And then nothing happens. And we wonder why the value of our work is always in question.

Here's the reality: our job isn't just to help them understand what we found. It's also to ensure they know what to do with it.

Same role, different mindset—one that you need to understand.

YOUR ROLE: THE GUIDE, NOT THE HERO

When you picked up this book and read the cover, you wanted to become a better data storyteller. But here's the reality: being a great data storyteller is not enough.

Now that you see the villains and the trap, you know it takes far more than communicating your findings "well" to be successful. You need influence. You need trust. You need to help drive decisions.

And to do that, you need to understand your role in the process. Sorry to disappoint, but you're not the hero of the story. Your data is not the hero. Your golden insights are not the hero.

There is one hero in the story—your stakeholders. They are the ones who make the decisions. They are the ones who are accountable for the outcomes.

Your role is the guide.

Not the "I have all the answers" genius man. Not the fixer with all the solutions. The guide.

We've created a generation of professionals who are brilliant at analysis but lost when it comes to being a guide—professionals who create decision readiness.

Decision readiness means stakeholders leave knowing exactly what to do next—and ready to do it.

When was the last time you walked out of a meeting knowing—without a doubt—that stakeholders were going to act on your recommendations? Rarely, if ever.

Think about *Iron Man*. When Tony Stark is trapped in that cave, he doesn't escape because of raw genius. He escapes because Yinsen guides him. Yinsen doesn't build the arc reactor or the flight suit. He doesn't make the final decision. He doesn't even survive.

But his presence, his words, his influence? Turned panic into purpose. Chaos into direction. And fear into action.

That is your role. You're Yinsen!

You set the stage for decisions to happen. You turn confusion into clarity. You turn disagreement into alignment. You surface emotions that create connection. You bring structure where everything feels chaotic.

You don't own the decision. You own the space that makes the decision possible. That is real influence.

When you stop trying to be the hero and start operating as the guide, everything changes—your presence, your confidence, your impact, even the way leaders respond to you.

> Knowing whether people are ready to act—that's what separates a traditional data storyteller from a decision driver. It's the skill that ensures stakeholders don't just understand your insights—they act on them. It's the "high-value" skill that gets you remembered, invited back to the room, and promoted.

Yes, everything we've learned in our careers so far matters too, but this is the accelerator. Decision drivers are the future.

That's the mindset shift I made—and the shift this framework will help you make too.

I used the Data Storytelling (4D) Framework to drive decisions. Now I'm going to show you how to do the same.

THE DATA STORYTELLING (4D) FRAMEWORK

Years ago, I was teaching a data visualization workshop in Australia. We were having so much fun—building dashboards, presenting them to the class, celebrating our great designs. The energy in the room was off the charts.

But something wasn't sitting right with me.

My students were obsessed with the design. . . and mostly ignoring the data. Dashboard designs? A+. The data being displayed? Solid C—at best.

I felt awful. I was the one teaching them how to do it.

I could barely sleep on the 17-hour flight back to the United States. I kept thinking about all the students I'd trained. All the dashboards that would never get used.

THE DATA STORYTELLING (4D) FRAMEWORK™

Here I was, the "dashboard queen." And I'd been teaching people how to make bad data look good.

Ugh.

Beautiful charts. Zero clarity. Zero alignment. Zero action.

That was my wake-up call.

A turning point in my career. It forced me to start to figure out not what looks good, but what actually drives action.

It took years of trial and error—watching what worked, and what failed, what created alignment, and what killed it. I read everything I could on behavioral science and tested what I learned with clients. Slowly, a pattern began to emerge.

That pattern became the Data Storytelling (4D) Framework (Figure 3.2).

1. **Discover:** Ask questions that uncover the real context.
2. **Define:** Build stories that create alignment.
3. **Design:** Create visuals that drive action.
4. **Deliver:** Present so they're ready to decide.

Four steps. One outcome: turn stakeholders from "great insight" to "how do we start?"

Let me show you how. This works whether you're a data analyst, leader, product manager, consultant, engineer, or business professional.

Figure 3.2   The Data Storytelling (4D) Framework

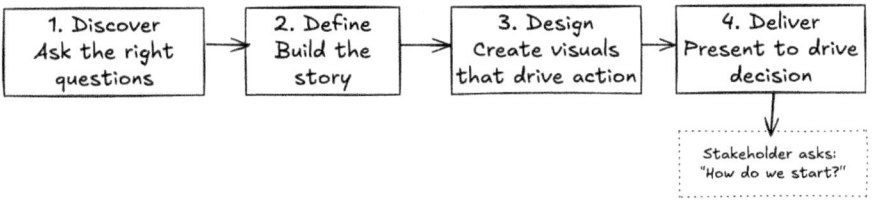

It works whether you're:

1. Presenting to executive committees
2. Walking someone through a dashboard
3. Running a QBR
4. Jumping into a last-minute meeting
5. Building a roadmap
6. Sending an async update

Same structure. Same steps. Same outcome: getting people from information to action. Fast.

Let me show you how each step works.

Step 1 → Discover: Ask the Right Questions

Great stories start by asking the right questions.

First, you need to understand the context of the story:

1. **The Who:** "Who do you picture using this?" The real users, not the leaders who delegate.
2. **The When:** "When do you picture needing this?" The true urgency, not manufactured pressure.
3. **The What:** "What triggered this request?" The real driver behind the request.

These questions give you the business context. Not the politically correct version. Not the corporate speak version. The human version.

Here's what we often forget:

When it comes to the *Who*, stakeholders are rarely the real end users. They request the work, but someone else has to actually use it. If that person is not in the room, you're already building blind.

Next is the *When*. Corporate urgency is often... theatrical. Everyone always says, "We needed it yesterday," even when the deadline is weeks away. You need the true deadline. It helps to prioritize your next steps.

Last is the *What*—"What triggered this request?" This uncovers the true motivation behind the requests. Not "We need a dashboard" but:

1. "If we don't get this under control soon, things could get ugly next quarter."
2. "A customer escalation landed on my desk this morning."
3. "The board is questioning our strategy."

These aren't the *why*. They're the *why now* of the request.

If you miss this, you risk building the right solution for the wrong audience at the wrong time. In some cases, you may discover they're not even ready for a solution.

This isn't just better requirements gathering.

This is the difference between being an order taker and becoming a strategic partner.

Step 1 gives you the context.

Step 2 uses the context to shape the story.

Step 2 → Define: Create Stories That Stick

Once you understand the context, you're ready to craft the story.

Help your stakeholders build a story they can agree on—not a random collection of metrics masked as KPIs, but a compelling data story everyone can actually follow and act on.

In California, I used our Data Storytelling Storyboard. As shown in Figure 3.3, it has four parts:

Figure 3.3 The Data Storytelling Storyboard

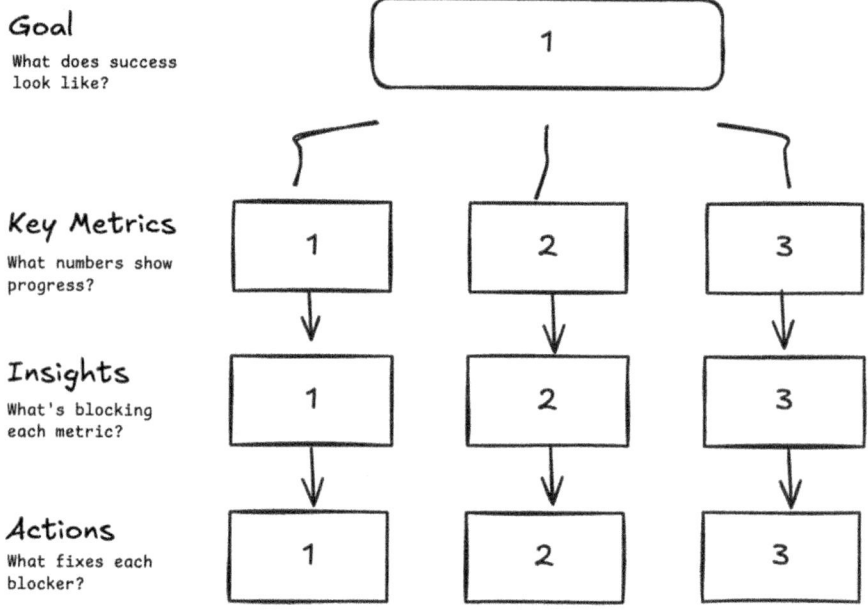

1. **The Goal (setup):** Define what success looks like—the North Star everyone can point to.
2. **The Key Metrics (rising tension):** The 3–5 numbers that show whether you're moving toward your goal.
3. **The Insights (conflict):** The blockers stopping these numbers from hitting their targets.
4. **The Actions (resolution):** The steps to remove each blocker.

The storyboard is your alignment engine. It cuts through the noise, hierarchy, and endless back-and-forth. It gives stakeholders a clear, shared way to organize their thinking and co-create solutions that actually make sense together. It gives you a tool to keep the conversation on track.

Everyone writes their answers on sticky notes. The storyboard organizes them. Any misalignments become instantly visible.

In California, it took about five minutes for them to spot the misalignment: different definitions of success. The storyboard didn't solve their problem—it made the real issue visible.

> You're not creating the story for them. You're guiding them to craft their own.

By the end of the Step 2, you have a compelling story, validated with data and signed off by the business.

Next, it's time for you to bring the story to life in Step 3.

Step 3 → Design: Create Visuals That Drive Action

Everyone's favorite step: design.

Now that you have the story, it's time to turn it into something stakeholders can actually use.

However, unlike traditional dashboards, story-driven dashboards guide decisions.

You're not building another report; you're bringing their story to life.

Story-driven dashboards display the Goal at the top. Decision tiles show each key metric with its insight and action. Figure 3.4 shows our story-driven dashboard template.

In Chapter 7, I'll show you how to create slide decks following the same four-part structure: Goal → Key Metrics → Insights → Actions. Same story. Different format. Same influence.

Figure 3.4 The Story-driven Dashboard Template

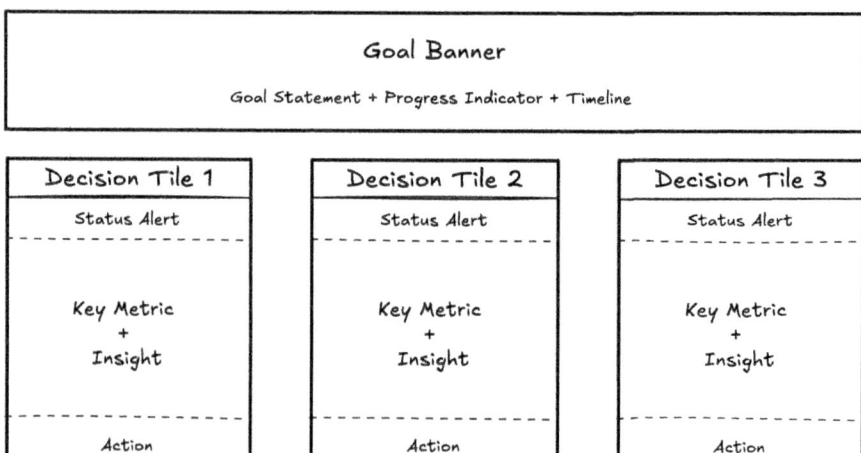

But the best data visualization in the world means nothing if you can't present it with influence and confidence. That's where Step 4 comes in—learning to deliver with confidence.

Step 4 → Deliver: Present to Win

This is where most data professionals stumble. They nail the data visualization but fumble the delivery. They have great insights but lose the audience's attention.

Step 4 changes that.

The story-driven presentation structure follows the same four-part structure: Goal → Key Metrics → Insights → Actions. Within five minutes, each part activates different brain networks (see Chapter 2).

Here's what happens:

THE DATA STORYTELLING (4D) FRAMEWORK™

1. **Goal:** They sync to your vision (prefrontal cortex engages).
2. **Key Metrics:** Their brain creates natural tension from the gap (anterior cingulate fires).
3. **Insights:** They feel the problem with you (limbic system activates).
4. **Actions:** Dopamine prints the solution in their memory (basal ganglia locks it in).

This sequence works because it follows how people naturally process stories. Instead of fighting against how the brain works, you're working with it.

In Chapter 8, I'll show you exactly how to deliver each part—what phrase to use, how to read the room in real time, and what to do when they push back.

The complete Data Storytelling (4D) Framework is your secret weapon to go from data presenter to decision driver.

THE MISSING PIECE

You've seen the Data Storytelling (4D) Framework in action. You've watched it create alignment in record time.

But I didn't tell you everything: I wasn't just using the 4D Framework; I was measuring whether it was working in real time.

Every nod, every question, and every shift in tone told me whether they were ready to move forward or not.

One day, a former Navy SEAL friend inspired me to look at stakeholders' meetings with a different lens. SEALs don't guess if someone is a threat—they observe, measure, and adjust.

What if influence worked the same way?

What if you could measure or even predict whether someone was going to act on your data while they were still talking?

I wasn't just using the Data Storytelling Framework that day in California.

I was measuring whether it was working—in real time.

Every nod. Every pronoun shift. Every timeline cue told me exactly where they stood.

The Push-and-Hope era of your career is officially over.

Chapter 4 shows you how to see what I saw.

And once you see it? You can't unsee it.

CHAPTER FOUR

THE THREE SIGNS OF INFLUENCE

"The most important thing in communication is hearing what isn't said."

—Peter Drucker

"Hi... sorry to drop in so late. I'm Coach Simmons. I got your email. Can you please walk me through this? There's a lot riding on this."

I looked up from my desk, gym bag on the floor, hoping to make it to the gym before they stopped serving that chopped salad I'd been craving since lunch. Instead, I found myself staring at one of the team's football coaches in the doorway of my tiny office.

He was holding a printed copy of the email I sent less than an hour ago—the final GPA report for our college football team.

From where I was sitting, he looked like a giant—his tone, calm but stern. I was less than three months out of college, a new data scientist in the university's statistics department, taking PhD classes at night while learning the job by day. This was my first big project, and I was not going to screw it up.

He lifted the paper slightly. "I just want to understand how you got to this number. It's coming in lower than expected—and I need to be sure we're looking at it correctly."

We were 0.2 points below the required average GPA—a tiny difference with massive consequences for funding, recruiting, and reputation. These scores were about to be reported to the major college magazines and *Forbes*.

I had spent weeks building and validating the model. Weeks combing through every line of SAS code. Weeks back and forth with my colleagues double-checking everything.

But none of that would change the fact that the number he needed wasn't the number I got.

I started walking him through the logic—step by step, line by line. He kept nodding as his eyes pierced the screen.

"Can we go through it again? I want to be absolutely sure," he asked again. "Let's see if Tammy is available as well." She was my boss.

Soon my tiny office had all hands on deck—everyone gathered around my tiny screen as I re-explained the same model, the same logic, the same math.

The more I explained, the more he questioned my model. He kept glancing at my boss, searching for an answer I clearly hadn't given—one closer to what he wanted to hear. Then the conversation took a sharp turn. He started asking about my background—how long I'd been in the role and whether I'd handled something this important before, which is just a polite way of questioning my credibility. (Sigh.) At that point, the humiliation had me looking for a hole in the wall to crawl into. Two hours and three full model reviews later, the number remained exactly the same. Don't shoot the messenger.

Years later, I realized there was nothing I could have said in that moment that would have gotten him to trust my result. His emotions had already made the decision before he walked into my office. He wasn't listening to understand; he was listening to hear what he wanted to hear—a GPA result that would protect the program. Period.

I wish I had understood that five minutes in. It would have saved me weeks of model revisions "with closer oversight," an impostor-syndrome hangover—all over a number that the data could not produce.

I wish I had known the signs—the ones that told me, *"No matter what you say, I'm not buying it."* I didn't know we weren't even having the same conversation.

But years later—once I learned the science of influence—I understood what happened: This wasn't a Mico failure. It wasn't a model failure. It was a clarity failure—because he had already chosen not to understand. And without clarity, he was never going to buy into my model or the result.

What happened in that tiny office took place long before I learned how to structure a story or guide a room. Back then, I didn't have any methods or frameworks—just models and numbers.

The numbers never changed, but I spent the next three days feverishly running variations of the model under "close oversight," each time hoping maybe, somehow, I'd come up with the result he wanted. I didn't.

What I did learn was a hard lesson: your insights are only as good as your stakeholder's readiness to receive them. No amount of technology or great design can overcome an emotional decision that has already been made.

That lesson cost me three sleepless nights and made me seriously question my future as a data scientist. I'm writing this chapter so it will never cost you the same.

PILLAR 2: SIGNALS

Looking back, I was too young and inexperienced to know what I was seeing. Outside of my algorithms and models, I had no idea how to convince someone that my numbers were right. I didn't even know how to tell the story.

I could read the data—but had zero understanding of how to read human behavior. I didn't know how to tell the difference between a polite nod and true clarity.

I thought influence was about having the right answer. It's not.

Influence starts by recognizing the signals in front of you—the ones that tell you if someone is genuinely engaging with your story or simply waiting for the meeting to end.

Remember Damasio's research from Chapter One? Decisions start with emotion. And emotions always leave signals—tiny, measurable micro-behaviors you can learn to see. They're like captions for what your stakeholders are really thinking—signals that tell you if someone is aligning with your idea or just listening along.

Once you learn to see these signals, everything changes. You stop guessing they "get it." You stop hoping "something sticks." You stop thinking, "Maybe I should've said it differently."

Pillar 1 gave you the structure—a way to build stories their brains can follow. Pillar 2 gives you the lens—a way to see, in real time, if your story is working.

Together they form the Buy-In Method—a simple system that helps you create influence and measure it in real time (Figure 4.1).

This is the part no one teaches—the part that quietly decides whether your story drives a decision or becomes another "nice presentation" everyone forgets by next week.

But first, we need to address another elephant in the room—one we can't ignore.

THE PEOPLE PROBLEM

There's a scene in *Moneyball* that lives rent-free in my head.

Billy Beane had data that could have revolutionized the baseball scouting industry. The problem? He couldn't get anyone to listen.

Figure 4.1 Buy-In Method details

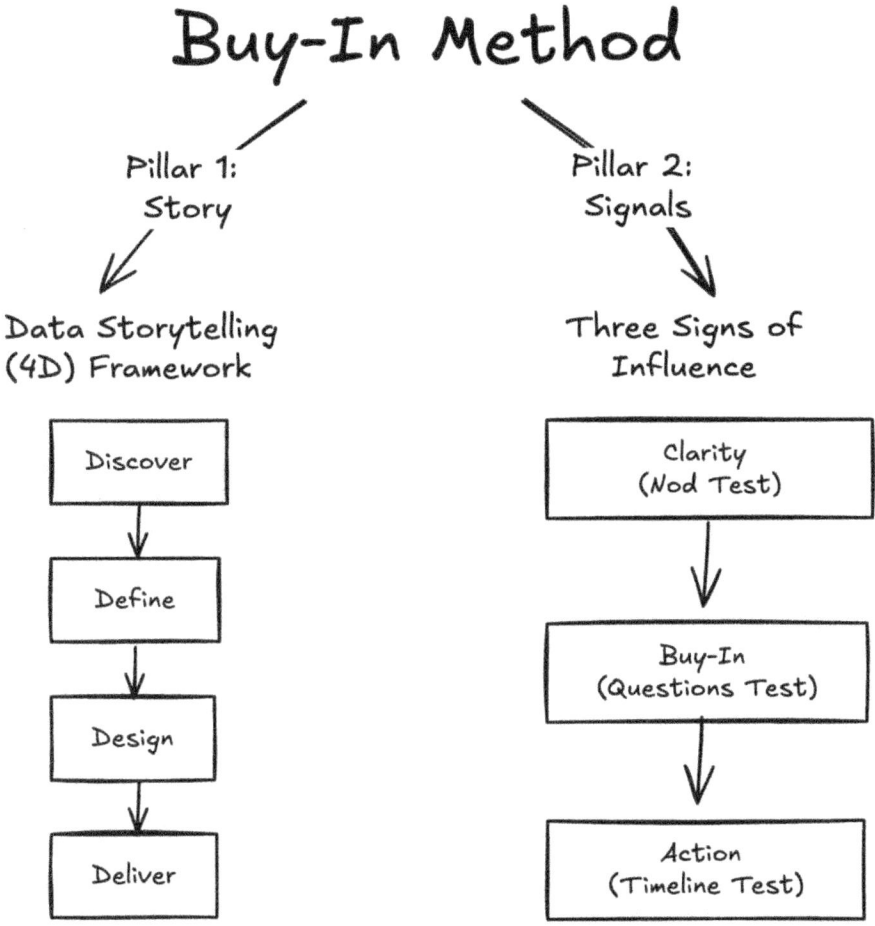

The older scouts kept dismissing his analytics with lines like "He doesn't look like a ballplayer" or "He doesn't pass the eye test." So they didn't trust him.

Meanwhile, other scouts—using far weaker methods—were winning over the older scouts simply because they knew how to speak their language.

Billy wasn't losing because his math was wrong. He was losing because he had no idea how to shift their thinking—how to move them away from the eye-test mentality.

He had the data. He had the story. He just didn't have the buy-in—and in that world, the gut beats math every time.

He was fighting a people problem, not a data problem.

And the more I replayed that scene, the more I realized something that made me very uncomfortable.

Many of us have lived that *Moneyball* moment. We have the data. We have the right models. We even have the truth. But none of it matters if the people in the room aren't ready to receive it.

Like Billy, we fail to read the room. We struggle to control the conversation. And that really bothered me.

As data professionals, we've always heard people whisper, "It's a people problem." But no one really ever explained what that actually meant. Was it that our stakeholders were the problem? Were we the problem?

"No." I was told. "It's the culture. It's how things are done around here."

But culture is just people's behavior on repeat. The people problem doesn't mean that humans are difficult. It's our expectations of how humans *should* behave that's the problem.

In a perfect world, we want them to think rationally, remove all bias, and send clear signals.

They don't. They respond to pressure, incentives, risks, and emotions.

We can't control their behavior. But we can measure it.

And before you roll your eyes—this isn't soft-skills training.

The moment you mention "reading people" or anything related to communication, everyone assumes you're heading to HR for role-playing exercises about difficult conversations—generic workshops designed for customer-service conflicts, not business professionals who need stakeholders to actually act on their insights.

This is something else entirely.

Top sales teams spend thousands on training to learn how to read buying signals, micro-expressions, and commitment language—it's called *decision science*. Executives go on expensive luxury retreats to learn the art of the deal.

Yet somehow, the folks who work with the most valuable asset in any organization—data—are winging its delivery and impact.

This penny-wise, pound-foolish mentality is killing our credibility. Organizations will spend $500,000+ on a dashboard that nobody uses but won't invest $5,000 to teach someone how to get stakeholders to act on it.

I'm tired of watching data professionals fail like I did.

Right now, most of us are measuring all the wrong things—dashboard views, clicks, logins, "time on slide," or "time on page"—and then wondering why no one is acting on our data.

> We're tracking engagement when we should be tracking readiness.

And that really bothered me.

WE'RE MEASURING THE WRONG THING

Think about your last "successful" dashboard launch. I bet you measured user logins, average time spent on the platform, and number of users.

Sorry to break it to you, but these metrics tell us nothing.

They're vanity metrics—IT-driven. They have no business impact. They serve more to CYA (cover your butt) than to help the business.

We're one of the only industries that build solutions, ship them, celebrate it, and have no idea if it actually worked. Meanwhile, the real decisions are happening in a completely different room.

While you're excited about 30+ minutes of average time spent on the platform, studies show that users spend 1.8 hours daily searching for information they can't find. That's roughly $1.7 million lost annually per 100 employees.

And yet—we're hyped about 250 logins last month.

The reality? Eighty percent of insights never deliver any business outcomes, while 68% of enterprise data goes completely unused. No wonder eight out of ten data projects fail.

Slide decks? Same problem. Death by bullet point is alive—and killing productivity and decision-making in companies everywhere.

Remember the $777 billion breakdown I mentioned in Chapter One? That's just what organizations spend on data talent and tools.

> The cost of not solving the people problem—the "data culture" gap— is over $3.1 trillion lost annually in the U.S. economy alone!

Not because of the tech. Because of humans.

The truth is simple:

- Dashboards don't drive decisions.
- Stories don't drive decisions on their own.
- People drive decisions.

We're spending billions of dollars on better tools and more technical training while completely ignoring whether any of it is used to make a decision.

Most of the time, we're not even in the room when the final decision is made. We have no way to measure whether action is taken, outside of seeing a positive change in the data later on. We don't see the follow-up meetings or know if our insights made it to the final call. We can't control whether they decide to finally act.

So what can we influence? What can we measure?

Stakeholder readiness—the likelihood that people in the room will take action.

Instead of waiting weeks to see if our insights make a difference, we could know what's going to happen before they even leave the room.

And when stakeholders are ready to take action, the business impact is huge.

Here's the proof: high-growth companies that track stakeholder decision readiness make three times more decisions than their competitors. Sales teams using similar methods show 34% annual revenue growth, while everyone else shows a measly 11%.

So how do you influence stakeholder readiness?

Not by forcing it, but by measuring it. And once you know what to look for, you can create the conditions for it to happen naturally.

Think of the Three Signs of Influence as a simple people metric—a way to track clarity, buy-in, and action in real time, the same way you track numbers on a dashboard.

They're already happening all around you; you just didn't know what to look for. Specific types of nods, questions, and timeline mentions show up in almost every meeting,

Let me show you what to look for—starting with your very next meeting.

THE THREE SIGNALS

Before going any further, one thing needs to be clear: this is not about manipulation. This isn't a sales script or a persuasion hack designed to push people into decisions they don't want to make.

The goal is to help you spot genuine signs of engagement that happen subconsciously—so that you can tell if someone has clarity, is bought in, and is ready to act.

> Your job isn't to force these signs. The Data Storytelling (4D) Framework should naturally trigger them.

And even if you're using other frameworks or methodologies, these signs still show up. You just need to know what to look for.

Your role is to create a safe space for the Three Signs to occur naturally, then measure if you're creating real buy-in. Because without buy-in, there is no action. You can't have one without the other.

The Three Signs of Influence always show up in the same order: clarity → buy-in → action.

Sign #1: Clarity—The Nod Test

This is the easiest sign to spot. You've probably seen dozens of nods in meetings this week.

Nods typically mean "yes" or "I'm with you." But yes to what, exactly?

- "Yes, sure—let's move on."
- "Yes, I understand what this really means."

They are not the same. The polite "Yes, sure—let's move on" nod is a social script. It keeps the meeting moving forward and protects people from looking confused. The "Yes, I understand what this really means"—the clarity nod—is the one you're looking for.

Researchers who study nonverbal behavior have found that when people truly grasp an idea, their body language shifts.

Here's how to spot the difference:

- **"Yes, sure" nods (polite gestures):** They're fast, robotic, and socially appropriate—think *Stepford Wives*. They usually lack eye contact and feel like empty acknowledgment, as the person is focused on the next activity.
- **"Yes, I understand" nods (clarity):** They're slower and more intentional—think Gordon Ramsay when he sees a good beef Wellington. They usually come with eye contact, a lean-forward, and a slight pause as they think.

Nods happen subconsciously—no tricks needed to trigger them. Someone either has clarity or they don't.

Most data professionals never learned to look for the difference. Any nod gets treated as buy-in. The results? Endless requirements sessions and "reply-all" email threads. They were confused, not on board.

In Chapters 5–8, you'll learn exactly how to spot real clarity nods and what to do when you don't see them. For now, just start to observe and ask yourself one question: "Are they nodding politely, or because they genuinely understand?"

Once you're confident you have Sign #1, you're ready to look for Sign #2.

Sign #2: Buy-In— The Questions Test

Spotting buy-in is a little bit trickier.

When people are engaged and starting to care, they ask questions—but not just any questions.

Most of us are so relieved to see engagement that we treat any question like a win. Soon after the meeting, the momentum evaporates, and we're back to square one.

Questions aren't just requests for more information; they reveal how the information you're sharing is being processed.

In one large study of 35,000 speed-dating chats by Harvard researchers, people who asked follow-up questions were significantly more likely to get second dates—not because they were polite but because their questions revealed real interest.

The same thing happens in business conversations. When people are genuinely bought in, their language patterns change. Their brains shift from observer to participant mode. Their questions move from "you/your" to "we/our," a clear sign of ownership. It's subconscious. They can't fake genuine emotional investment.

Here's what low or no buy-in sounds like:

- **Confusion:** "Wait, what does this mean, exactly?" (*I don't even understand what you're proposing.*)
- **Curiosity:** "That's interesting—how did you come up with this?" (*Cool idea, but I'm not invested yet.*)
- **Skepticism:** "Are you sure this will work?" (*Prove it to me first, buddy.*)
- **Analytical:** "What's the ROI on this?" (*I'm analyzing, not emotionally connecting.*)
- **Comparative:** "How does this compare to what we're doing now?" (*I'm still evaluating my options.*)

They're thinking and evaluating, but they're not emotionally investing yet.

Now listen to high buy-in questions:

- "How would *we* implement this?" (*I'm mentally joining your solution.*)
- "What would *our* timeline look like?" (*I'm planning our future together.*)

- "Who on *our* team would need to be involved?" (*I'm allocating our people.*)
- "When could *we* start this?" (*I'm ready to move.*)
- "What would *we* need to do first?" (*I'm committed to action.*)

Same meeting. Same deck. Completely different questions.

That tiny pronoun shift—from "you/your" to "we/our"—is your signal that they've stepped into the story with you. They've moved from watching your idea to picturing themselves living in it. In data terms, they've stopped treating your information like a report and started treating it like part of their strategy.

In Chapters 5–8, you'll learn how to spot these ownership questions and what to do when you don't hear them.

For now, start listening for that shift. When they say "we", buy-in has begun.

Sign #3: Action— The Timeline Test

Clarity and buy-in are powerful, but they're still not the finish line. Here comes the moment of truth: are they going to do something?

This is where 99% of professionals quietly check out. After some nods of congruence and a few engaging questions, they pack up and move on to the next project.

You're right. It's their job to make the final call. But it's still your job to do everything you can to ensure they're ready. And there is a simple way to read this.

Listen for one simple signal: time.

Not just any mention of time—a future timeline.

When people start talking about "when," their brains have shifted from *buy-in mode* ("Should we do this?") to *action mode* ("When will we do this?") Robert Cialdini's research on influence shows this increases the likelihood of taking action by 400%. Yes, 400%! Kind of crazy for such simple words. Even more important, the brain also does this subconsciously. It's not easily faked.

Here's what high action readiness sounds like:

- "When could we start this?"
- "How long would this take?"
- "Next month we could. . ."
- "By Q2, we should have this in place."
- "Tomorrow, I'll share this with my team."

Once they start adding real dates and timeframes, their brains have just switched into implementation mode.

The strongest action signal is when time and ownership show up together:

- "When *we* implement this. . ."
- "Next week *we* could. . ."
- "*We* should start soon. . ."

This signals that your recommendations, insights, or ideas have moved from "interesting" to "ours."

When they're not ready, the language gets vague:

- "When we have time. . ."
- "Eventually, this may become useful."
- "Someday, we should look at this."
- "Maybe next year. . ."

Translation: Not happening. The chances of action are close to zero. No concrete timeline mention, no real commitment.

But it's not just about randomly spotting the three signs. What really changes the game is when they show up together.

THE SEQUENCE MATTERS

The Three Signs of Influence are not a checklist. It isn't a buffet where you grab whatever looks good. The order matters. When the sequence breaks, so does the decision.

I've seen this play out hundreds of times:

No clarity → no buy-in

If they don't clearly understand what you're asking them to do—and why it matters to THEM—there's a slim chance they're getting on board.

Damasio showed us emotions drive decisions. But emotions need something to connect to. When stakeholders are fuzzy on the problem, your suggestions or the "what's in it for me (WIIFM)," they can't emotionally invest.

> No clarity means no emotional hook—and without that hook, there's no buy-in. Period.

No buy-in → no action.

They get it. They like it. They want it. But no one puts a stake in the ground to move forward—no dates, no owners, no budget. Everyone leaves the meeting, other fires show up, their calendar fills up, and just like that your suggestions get demoted to the "back burner."

This is the Push-and-Hope trap we discussed in Chapter 3.

Any of these signs can make a meeting feel successful, but seeing all three signs in order is the game-changer (Figure 4.2):

Clarity: The nod shows they see what you're saying.

Buy-in: The "we/us" questions show they've stepped into the story.

Action: The timeline mention shows they're ready to act on the story.

Figure 4.2   Three Signs of Influence sequence

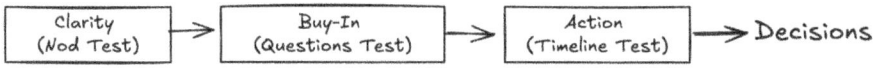

When you see all three signals in this order, that's when decisions become real.

Fellow data professionals, this matters more to us than almost any other professionals. Why? We don't control the decision. We don't control the budget. We don't control the politics.

But now, we have a people metric we can trust. It keeps us honest and on track when it comes to driving decisions forward with our data.

If we don't see all three signs in this order, we know exactly where the decision has stalled, and where to focus next.

You don't need perfection. You need practice. You just shifted from hoping to measuring. From data storyteller to decision driver.

DECISION DRIVERS

Decision drivers are a different breed.

For executives reading this: your team already has the technical skills. What they're missing is this people metric—a way to know if their insights are going to be used before the meeting ends.

You don't stop being a data storyteller when you become a decision driver. You just level up.

Data storytellers focus on crafting the perfect narrative. Decision drivers craft the narrative and read the room to see if it's landing.

We still care about telling compelling stories with our dashboards, reports, and slide decks—but we know those are just tools. They're not magically going to get up and drive our stakeholders to act.

That's why we also track people metrics.

Here is what we ask ourselves:

Traditional Data Storyteller	Decision Driver
Was it clear?	Are they nodding?
Did they like it?	Did I hear "we" and "our" in their questions?
Will they act?	Did anyone attach a timeline to the next step?

See the difference?

> Traditional data storytellers measure outputs. Decision drivers measure readiness.

Pillar 1 gives you the structure—a way to build stories their brains can follow.

Pillar 2 gives you the lens—a way to measure your influence in real-time.

Together, they form the Buy-In Method.

In the next four chapters, I'm going to show you exactly how to use this system:

How to design dashboards, reports and slide decks that naturally trigger all Three Signs of Influence. What to do when things don't go as planned. How to turn every stakeholder meeting into an opportunity to grow your influence.

You're not just telling better data stories.

You see what others miss. You measure what others guess. You influence what others hope for.

You're now a decision driver.

Let's get to work.

CHAPTER FIVE

DISCOVER—ASK THE RIGHT QUESTIONS

"The art and science of asking questions is the source of all knowledge."

—Thomas Berger

Growing up in a small Caribbean island, I heard a lot about New York from my mom. It was a bucket list item.

So when I got the call to take the lead on the dashboard design for a big pharmaceutical company, I was both shocked and petrified.

"Someone sent me one of your dashboards. We could use your help up here. We have a software deal in the mix, and we really need the wow factor."

I played it cool. I asked a few questions, negotiated my rate like it mattered—knowing fully well I was getting on that plane the next week.

Monday morning, I walked into my first requirements-gathering session fresh and excited. Laptop, notepad, and pen. Ready to wow them.

I had no idea what would happen next.

When I walked into that conference room, I was touted as the dashboard designer whose POC (proof of concept) would get the software deal closed. But I saw the surprise on their faces—young woman, Caribbean accent, Asian name. I clearly wasn't what they expected.

In that moment, I knew I had no margin for error. I had to figure out how to get context and build trust fast—or this would be my first and last New York project.

The room was packed with stakeholders. After the introductions, I smiled and opened with what I thought was the perfect question: "So, what are you guys trying to achieve here? Walk me through it."

Pure chaos ensued.

So I tried to tighten it up. "Okay. Maybe that was too open-ended. I see some of you have reports printed out. What do you want to see on the dashboard?"

More chaos.

Then the guy on the left grabbed a marker and started drawing on the whiteboard. I stepped back, relieved. Finally, someone who knew what they wanted.

He never finished. Everyone kept interrupting: add this, remove that, change that, make it more like this. And suddenly, we were five minutes over.

"Alright, we're running over," I said. "Let's continue this on Thursday. Thanks for your time."

I wanted to rip off my badge, spring out the door, and pretend I'd never heard the words "dashboard design lead."

What had just happened?

That was session one. Session two, three, four, and five? Even worse.

Two weeks in, I was exhausted. I had pages of notes, thirty KPIs, and a bunch of requests that started with "I want to see. . ." and ended with nothing actionable.

The Head of Research sent his entire team, yet no one had a clear idea of what he wanted or needed.

The project eventually got delivered, but I felt defeated. I was new to the Big Apple, and it felt like New York was about to spit me out.

That became my turning point: figure it out or pack up and go home.

Out of desperation, I called one of my mentors.

And the answer stung: The issue wasn't my stakeholders. It was me.

I was asking the wrong questions—and I didn't even know it.

Hindsight is expensive. In retrospect, I had two problems.

One, I had no idea what questions to ask.

Two, I had no idea how to ask them.

Before stepping into that room, I didn't know to ask:

Who is this really for? I just took whoever they thought should be in the room without vetting who needed to be there. This cost me time, momentum, and part of my sanity.

What triggered the request? I was told, "The Head of Research needs visibility into cost ahead of budget season," and I ran with it. That told me absolutely nothing about the real motivation. It turned out no one in the room knew, either.

When was it due? I came in being told, "It was due yesterday." But three months later, I was stuck on the requirements-gathering treadmill. The urgency turned out to be corporate speak—not a real deadline. Ugh.

If any of this sounds familiar—you're not broken. Your process is.

What I didn't understand yet was that even good questions can fail—if they engage only half the brain.

I thought I was gathering requirements, but what I was really gathering was random opinions.

Then I discovered a different type of question—dual-channel questions—questions that engage both sides of the brain at once.

They don't just get you answers. They get you context. Clarity. Buy-in. In one meeting instead of ten.

If you've ever walked out of a requirements session feeling defeated, this chapter is for you.

Before we get to the three questions, we need to understand why the questions we're trained to ask continue to fail us.

WHY YOUR QUESTIONS ARE FAILING YOU

In *The Ask Method*, Ryan Levesque drops a truth that every data person should tattoo into their brain: "Direct questions fail, because people often don't know what they truly want."

Henry Ford said it more bluntly: "Ask people what they want and they'll ask for faster horses."

That was me in New York—asking "good" questions and getting vague, useless answers.

Here's what nobody taught us: the brain processes information through two distinct channels.

- **The verbal (logic) channel:** Think words, language, abstract concepts
- **The imagery (visual) channel:** Think pictures, scenes, mental movies

When your questions trigger only one channel, you get half an answer. That's what I was doing when I asked:

- What do you want to see? → Logic-only. Answer: "Everything!"
- What do you want to measure? → Logic-only. Answer: "A long list of metrics"
- What do you want it to look like? → Visual-only. Answer: "Make it pretty."

None of those answers will tell you what matters.

Not because your stakeholders are being difficult—but because your questions are only talking to half of their brain.

Logic-only questions invite opinions.
Visual-only questions invite imagination.
Neither forces clarity.

Dual-channel questions work because they do something different: they make people think and picture at the same time.

For example: "What does success look like in 90 days?"

- **"What"** = forces a clear answer (logic)
- **"success"** = defines winning and pictures it (both)
- **"look like"** = runs a quick mental movie (visual)
- **"90 days"** = pins that movie to a specific moment (both)

Now you're not guessing—you're getting context.

And context is what separates projects that move forward and succeed from those that move forward and fail.

There are three questions that tell you—fairly quickly—whether a project is ready or headed for trouble.

Now that you understand how dual-channel questions work, let me give you three that will change how you kick off every project forever.

STEP 1: DISCOVER—YOU NEED CONTEXT FIRST

Here's what I wish someone had told me before I walked into that New York conference room:

You can't build the right story if you don't know the real story.

And you won't get the real story by jumping straight into requirements. You need three pieces of context first:

- *Who* is this really for?
- *When* do they need it?
- *What* triggered this request?

These questions would've saved me weeks of rework in New York.
They'll save you from projects that shouldn't even exist.
So many data projects skip these questions—and they fail.
But when you do ask them, the impact can be immediate.

One of our customers in the UK learned this approach and decided to try it the very next day—on a single project he was kicking off—to see if it worked. As soon as they started to dig in, it became painfully clear to everyone in the room, that the project wasn't ready. No one could name a clear end user. No one could agree on the real deadline. And when asked who would own the actual outcome, the room went silent.

The project was stopped, saving the company millions.

It wasn't blocked. It just wasn't ready.

The impact was big enough that they made a rule for every project: no data project would move forward until they had answers to the three Discovery questions first.

Studies show that 39% of project failures are caused by poor discovery.

Discovery is intentionally fast and low-touch. You do it before you build anything. Ask the three questions in one conversation (email, DM, or meeting)—and you're done. It also builds trust before you ask for anything.

Every step in the Data Storytelling (4D) Framework has two parts.

- **A tool:** What you use
- **A technique:** How you use it

For Discovery:

- **The tool:** The three questions
- **The technique:** How you ask them with dual-channel language

The following sections discuss the three questions.

Three Discovery Questions That Reveal Readiness

Question 1—*Who* do you picture using this?

Why this wording works:

- **"Who"** engages their logical channel; they think about specific people.
- **"do you picture using this"** activates their visual channel; they see real humans doing real work.

You're combining a logical cue ("Who") with a visual cue ("picture"), forcing both channels to engage instead of hiding behind vague, logic-only questions.

What you're really learning: Who will actually use your work—not just who asked for it. If your Three Signs of Influence are green, the response should sound like this:

Green-flag responses name real users, clear ownership, and a shared sense of responsibility.

They sound like this: "Joanne handles our Monday reports, and Mike in operations needs the production data. We really need to resolve this reporting bottleneck—it's been a constant headache for the entire team."

What to watch for:

- **Clarity (the nod test):** Nodding while naming users and a specific data point or timeframe
- **Buy-in (the question test):** Shift to "we/us" language in their follow-up questions

At this stage, you're not trying to start the project yet. You're checking if it's even ready to start. Big difference.

That's why you only watch for two signals:

- **Clarity:** Do they have clear answers?
- **Buy-in:** Are they emotionally invested?

Action comes later—during storyboarding in Chapter 6—when you're actually driving your stakeholders toward decisions.

Right now, you just need to know if they're ready. If you don't see the two signals, stop and course-correct before wasting everyone's time.

- "Most of the team" = shared usage, no primary end users
- "The business" = corporate jargon, no real users
- "Sales/Marketing/HR/Operations" = multiple audiences, no clear user

When I first started, as an introvert, I asked logic-only questions like "Who is this for?" or "Who will be using this?"

They felt efficient but triggered generic responses like "The sales team."

Those are red flags!

The dual-question format fixes this by forcing specificity. It pushes people to name real users, real deadlines, and concrete triggers—breaking abstraction and forcing clarity.

If you hit a red flag (a purely logical response), follow up with:

"Beryl, who specifically do you picture opening this when things hit the fan?"

That visual phrase—"when things hit the fan"—makes it almost impossible to give a vague answer. They have to picture a real person, at a real moment, doing real work.

Once you're clear on who this is really for, you're ready to learn the timing. Because knowing who needs it means nothing if you don't know when it's actually needed.

Question 2—*When* do you see this being needed?

Why this exact wording works:

- **"When"** engages the logical channel (they think about time and constraints).
- **"do you see this being needed"** activates the visual channel (they picture the moment the data actually matters).

What you're really learning: the real deadline versus perceived urgency.

Green-flag responses tie a specific date to consequences and personal stakes. You want a solid month and day, even if it's an estimate.

"The board meeting is March 15, and if we don't have clean numbers by then, the hard questions start. We need to be ready at least a week before then."

What to watch for:

- **Clarity:** You see immediate nods as they name a real deadline tied to the project.
- **Buy-in:** They start asking follow-up questions using "we/us" language that references consequences, timing, and next steps.

Here's how this sounds in a real conversation:

You're listening for whether timing is tied to a real, specific business event or deadline—or just a request that sounds urgent.

Red flag responses float to the surface.

- "ASAP"/"Soon"/"End of month" = time without an event; more of a placeholder
- "Leadership wants it" = someone else's deadline
- "It's urgent" = generic pressure

If you hit a red flag, follow up with a question like:

"Rupert, what do you *see* happening if we miss the board meeting?"

That will push their brain to visualize the actual consequence (visual channel) and connect the deadline to real business impact. If they can't answer, the urgency is not real.

The goal isn't to pin down a perfect date. It's to surface a real business deadline—one tied to an actual business event. Without that, the project can drag on forever. I've watched it happen on repeat.

Now that you've got a user and a deadline, it's time to find out why this landed on someone's desk. What's the real story behind the request?

Question 3—*What* is the story behind this?

Why this exact wording works:

- **"What is the story"** engages the logical channel (they think about events and facts).
- **"behind this"** activates the visual channel (they replay what actually happened).

What you're really learning: the trigger—the events that drove the request.

Green-flag responses describe what happened—a specific failure, conversation, or pressure point that created the need for the project.

Picture last quarter's board meeting. Someone asks a basic question: "What's our revenue looking like?" You freeze. You shuffle through a few reports on your laptop. The numbers don't match! You can't come up with a solid answer—while everyone waits. As the meeting ends, the Head of Sales pulls you aside and says, "We need to get our act together. We should have those revenue numbers ready to go." That's what landed this project on your desk.

And that's the story you need to hear when you ask Question 3.

What to watch for:

- **Clarity:** You'll see nods as they remember the real pressure behind the request—a decision, a problem, a miss, or a moment of accountability.
- **Buy-in:** They start asking "we/us" questions as they reveal personal stakes ("We'll embarrass ourselves," for example).

Here's how this shows up in real conversations:

You're listening for history. If there's no story, there's usually no real urgency.

Here are some red-flag responses to watch for:

- "It's a strategic initiative" = not tied to a real event
- "Leadership asked for it" = pressure without an actual cause
- "We just need visibility"/"single source of truth" = no consequence, no real reason

Those answers explain that a request exists—but not why. That's an issue.

If you run into one of these red flags, follow up with:

"Bernice, what *exactly* happened that *landed* this on your desk?"

The question forces the brain to recall the exact event that led to the request.

Here's the pattern. Each question reveals something different:

- Who → ownership
- When → urgency
- What → context

If you get an abstract answer for any of these, pause.

Projects don't fail because of a bad dashboard or report. Many times, they fail the readiness test, and we simply move forward and build anyway.

THE THREE DISCOVERY QUESTIONS IN ACTION

"We're hemorrhaging money on this project," Jennifer said, sliding a thick folder across the conference table. "The CEO wants a dashboard that shows her everything. Make it pretty."

I could feel my stomach drop. Another "show me everything" request. But this time, I had my three questions ready.

"Jennifer, quick question. Besides our CEO, who do you picture actually using this report when it's ready?"

She paused. Her shoulders softened. "Honestly? Me. I need it. Every Monday at 7 a.m., when I'm prepping for the executive team meetings, I get asked a lot of tough questions. I'm scrambling through five different reports trying to find answers, and half the time I'm making educated guesses."

Now we were getting somewhere, I thought.

"Okay, sorry to hear that. When do you see needing this by?"

"Yesterday would be nice," she laughed sarcastically. "But realistically? We have board prep in three weeks. I need solid numbers."

"What's the story behind all these Monday morning fire drills?"

That's when Jennifer's face dropped completely. "Last month, the board asked a simple question about customer retention. I had to say, 'I'll get back to you on that'—in front of everyone. Our CEO pulled me aside afterward and said we need to get our act together."

In seven minutes, we went from the CEO supposedly saying "show me everything" to helping Jennifer avoid Monday morning fire drills and never embarrass herself in front of the board again.

Dual-channel questions turn abstract requests into human stories.

The hidden truth: every vague request is someone's professional pain in disguise.

- "Show me everything" = "I'm lost and scared to admit it."
- "Make it pretty" = "I don't know what success looks like."
- "ASAP" = "I'm under pressure and need help."

Your three questions don't just provide context—they offer a safe space to be honest about what is needed.

WHY THESE QUESTIONS WORK

You just learned three Discovery questions. Now let me show you exactly how they work—and why the questions you were trained to ask keep failing.

Scientists call it *dual coding*. I call it "smart brain activation."

Before I explain the science, let's prove how it works on *your* brain.

1. Get a piece of paper and a pen (or open a note on your phone).
2. Write each of the following *visual* words, then draw the first picture that comes to mind below each one. After each drawing, hide it by scrolling down or turning over the paper.
   - Grow
   - Watch
   - Guard
3. Do the same thing for corporate jargon—write the word, draw the first picture that comes to mind below it, then hide each drawing.
   - Increase
   - Deploy
   - Govern
4. Now look at your drawings.

For the visual words, I bet you drew actual things—a camera, eyes watching, or a person observing, or a security guard or someone protecting something.

For the corporate jargon words, you probably either drew nothing, struggled with meaningless arrows, or stared at the page, confused. "Govern" probably left you completely blank.

How do I know? Because in my workshops, most attendees draw the exact same patterns. I'm not a mind reader—I just understand which words trigger your imagery networks.

Did you feel it?

This is why stakeholders zone out when you say, "Let's leverage our core competencies" (some even sigh heavily), but then lean forward with a nod when you say, "Let's picture success."

You just felt what your users feel: which words activate the brain, and which ones shut it down. That's your first superpower.

Figure 5.1 shows what's actually happening in the brain.

Figure 5.1 The brain's two information-processing channels—verbal (logic) and imagery (visual)

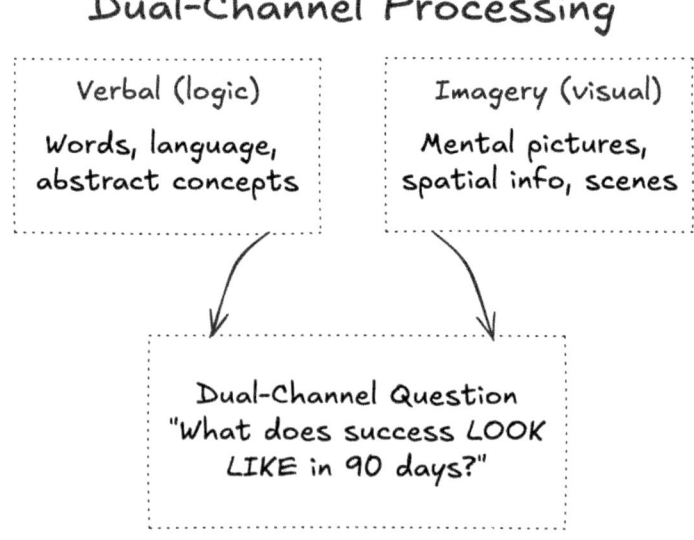

Visual words activate your memory and emotion networks. They pull from your real-life experiences, creating a mental movie.

Jargon words activate nothing—they are complete brain-dead zones. Your brain literally has no image to attach to these abstract concepts; as a result, you draw a blank. Remember what happened when you tried to visualize the word "govern"?

Our brains process information through two distinct channels.

- **The verbal (logic) channel:** Think words, language, and abstract concepts
- **The imagery (visual) channel:** Think pictures, scenes, and mental movies

When you ask logic-only questions, you get logic-only fluff.
For example:

- **"What"** = not an issue; forces clarity
- **"do you want"** = triggers random opinions
- **"to measure"** = opens the door to "everything that could matter"

So you get answers like:

- "We measure churn and retention."
- "Margin is really important."
- "We've always looked at user ratings."

None of these vague replies reveal the why or the true need.

On the other side of the brain, you have the visual channel. When you ask someone a purely visual question like "Can you draw what you want the dashboard to look like?" here is how the brain processes it:

- **"Can you "** = not the issue; it's an invitation
- **"draw + look like"** = visual trigger (shifts the brain into picture/layout mode)

- **"what you want"** = invites opinion, not purpose
- **"the dashboard"** = pushes solutions before understanding

Nothing in these questions asks what matters.
Nothing asks why it matters.
Nothing asks what decision this is meant to support.
So you get answers like:

- "I see everything running smoothly."
- "I picture having happy customers."
- "I can see us growing."

These answers aren't wrong—they're just incomplete.

They engage only the imagination- and emotion-side of the brain and lack any analytical structure. They're feelings and dreams, not inputs for decisions.

That's why the who, when, and what questions work—they don't just ask for information. They force the brain to think and picture at the same time. Logic + imagery. Facts + feelings. *Both* channels firing at once.

That's not some hocus-pocus trick. It's dual-coding by design.

And that's when you finally get the good stuff: facts plus feelings, in one shot. Not just what they want. But why they care.

Dual-channel questions build trust and show empathy. They don't just keep the conversation on track; they get to the real *why* up front.

But there's a catch.

A big part of asking the right questions is keeping the language "human"—and most of us were trained to do the opposite.

We have an unlikely enemy: corporate jargon. It's the language we get praised for at work. . . and now we have to unlearn.

Corporate jargon is death to the brain.

I teach my students, "We have to be untrained. We've been taught to sound professional—but it's costing us. Time. Results. Trust. We're not getting through to people. We're speaking *at* them, not *to* them."

Corporate jargon is the enemy of clarity. It's abstract. It's foggy. And it shuts the brain down.

Some of the top brain-dead corporate-jargon offenders include:

Say This (Dual-Coded)	Not This (Jargon)
"What would help us *grow* this quarter?"	"How can we *increase* performance?"
"What should we *cut* this month?"	"How do we *streamline* this?"
"How should we *frame* our approach?"	"What's our *strategic* approach?"
"What resources could we *unlock* immediately?"	"How can we *leverage* our resources?"
"What does success *look like* in 90 days?"	"How do we *benchmark* success?"
"What would *boost* our performance quickly?"	"How do we *optimize* performance?"

> Full cheat sheets and word guides are available by visiting drivingbuyin.com

Notice the pattern? Dual-channel questions use visual verbs like grow, unlock, boost, frame, and cut plus visual triggers like "look like." Jargon uses abstract verbs that your brain can't picture.

I don't know who taught us these "safe" corporate words, but we need to unlearn them—fast. It's literally killing careers.

Don't just stop saying these useless words—stop putting them in your reports, dashboards, slide decks, DMs, and emails.

Here's how people react to corporate jargon:

- **Kills curiosity:** People tune out.
- **Creates confusion:** No one knows what you actually mean.
- **Sounds robotic:** It breaks the human connection.

Now that you know why the three questions work—and what kills them, you spot corporate jargon and replace it with words that wake up the brain.

But here's the thing: conversations don't go as planned. Let's see how to fix that.

WHEN THE QUESTIONS DON'T WORK

Here is another unpopular truth: sometimes Discovery reveals a bigger issue—control. I'm not talking about vague answers. I'm talking about stakeholders who don't want clarity... they want compliance.

I'm talking about stakeholders who cross their arms and issue orders like they're in a military camp. They leave no room for input, insights, or innovation. They have a set vision in mind and just want you to execute it.

They see discovery as a waste of time.

They're easy to recognize:

- Little to no eye contact when asked questions
- Defensive body language
- Vague answers that don't improve no matter how you rephrase the question
- No shift to "we/us" language, remaining stuck in "I/me" for the entire conversation

If the discovery questions don't yield clear answers and you see zero buy-in, the project isn't ready. Period. Stop and escalate. That's strategic, not failure.

But that's rare.

Most of the time, vague answers aren't a sign of resistance—they're just misaligned brain channels.

As a data storyteller, you don't just ask better questions—you also know how to spot when things aren't working and course-correct quickly.

There are two reasons conversations go off track:

First, your questions shift off course. Even when you know the right questions, pressure and habits can hijack your wording. You slip into different modes and clarity disappears.

Second, your stakeholders get stuck in one channel. They answer with pure logic (lists of metrics or technology) or visual responses ("make it pretty") instead of engaging both.

Let me show you how to fix both.

Watch for mode shifts—this is where most people slip.

Mode shift can happen at any time—especially under pressure. Your questions can get hijacked by habit. Be careful not to let one of these modes take over:

- **Problem-solver mode:** Adding "…and what problem will this help them to solve? → This pulls you into diagnosis too early.
- **Order-taker mode:** Adding "…so I can make sure it's set up exactly how they want it? → This shifts you into pleasing the requester instead of understanding.
- **Overthinker mode:** Asking multiple questions at once. "Who do you see using this, and what does their Monday morning look like when they need it?" → Clarity gets buried.

The goal isn't to perfect the wording. It's to notice when a mode pulls your question off course. If you hear yourself adding "and..."—stop. Return to the original question.

This applies to all three discovery questions.

Now, here's how to fix the "vague answers" when stakeholders get stuck in one channel.

When you get a vague answer, here's the pattern that works every time: add their name plus the words "specifically" or "exactly" to any question.

For example:

- **Vague "who" response:** "Everyone will use it."
- **Recovery:** "Sarah, who specifically do you picture using this day-to-day?"
- **Vague "when" response:** "We need it soon."
- **Recovery:** "Mike, when exactly do you see needing this ready?"
- **Vague "what" response:** "It's a strategic initiative."
- **Recovery:** "Lisa, what specifically happened that made this land on your desk?"

Using someone's name cuts through mental noise and grabs their attention. Adding words like "specifically" or "exactly" makes it hard to stay abstract. The structure of the question doesn't change—it's the same structure, just delivered with more precision.

The pattern works for everything—but it's especially critical in virtual meetings, where it's even hard to read the room.

While face-to-face meetings create nine significant cues, virtual meetings create only one (Riedl et al., Scientific Reports, 2023). That's an 89% drop in how our brains sync up—a key component of building trust, empathy, and connection. No wonder the RTO (return-to-office) push after COVID was so aggressive.

When a virtual session goes sideways, here's what to do:

- **Sudden muting:** DM them: "Can you share your thoughts in chat?"
- **Camera off:** Ask: "Should we take a quick break or continue?"
- **Chat-only replies:** Say: "Feel free to type answers—I'll share anonymously if that helps."

While most professionals panic when meetings go off track, you now have a simple formula to fix it: use their name, add specificity, and watch your clarity return.

YOUR UNFAIR ADVANTAGE

You now have an unfair advantage.

If you've ever felt that quiet tension in a meeting—where something feels off but you can't quite name it—this is what you've been missing.

It's not confidence.

It's not seniority.

It's not better charts.

It's knowing how to check for project readiness—before you build, before you commit, before you burn time trying to fix the wrong problem.

You've mastered the three discovery questions, you know how to read clarity and buy-in in real time, and you know how to course-correct when conversations drift—whether you're in a conference room or on a screen.

You're no longer hoping the project goes well. You're putting your stakeholders through a quick litmus test before putting in any effort. It's the ultimate CYA (cover your butt) move.

That's not an order-taker move. That's a Decision Driver move. And that's what separates you from every other professional walking into a meeting with crossed fingers and a slide deck.

∧∧

And here's the part AI won't save you from: forcing human clarity when it doesn't exist.

That New York conference room taught me something I'll never forget: when you don't have margin for error, you learn to ask the right questions fast. These three gave me more than clarity. They gave me credibility—when I didn't "look the part."

But discovery is just context.

Jennifer's seven-minute conversation gave me everything I needed to know. But context alone doesn't make stakeholders act.

I had the who, the when, and the what. What I didn't have yet was the story that would make her say, "Yes, let's do this."

Chapter 6 shows you how to transform that narrative into a compelling story that truly drives decisions.

You just learned how to find out what matters. Now let's turn it into action.

CHAPTER SIX

DEFINE— STORIES THAT STICK

"The single biggest problem in communication is the illusion that it has taken place."

—George Bernard Shaw

The CFO slammed a thick binder on the conference table.

"Our KPIs," she announced. "All 140 of them."

Here I was, sitting across from the CFO of a major telecom provider, as her Head of Finance was about to defend why the senior team needed to track 140 metrics to "cover the entire business." Not 14. Not 40. One hundred and forty.

Unsurprisingly, their meetings had devolved into "who can define the metric" debates. That's why I was there.

"We track all of these," she insisted, flipping through the thick binder. "Customer acquisition. Network performance. Revenue per tower. Call drops. Employee satisfaction. . .." The list went on.

Everyone nodded in agreement.

You could see the sense of pride in the room. That binder had been their North Star for a decade. Nobody dared question it.

The reality? With 140 metrics, they likely weren't tracking anything beyond maybe the first five. They were drowning in information, starving for insights.

As I randomly opened the binder in the middle, I started to ask questions about the metrics on the page. Nobody could tell me what the metrics were, why they mattered, or how they connected to their goals. They spent more time arguing about the data than acting on it.

Their KPI binder was nothing more than classic "data comfort food": the feeling that more numbers equal more control. The emotion is real; the control is not.

Their senior leadership team was convinced that 140 metrics "covered the entire business," when, in reality, a few key KPIs and a handful of sharp insights are what actually drive action. The rest just fed information overload and analysis paralysis—exactly what they were trying to fix.

Feeling a bit overwhelmed, I went back to my hotel room that night and spread the binder out on my desk. I'd never seen so many KPIs in my life. What I thought would take an evening turned into three brutal days—highlighting, cross-referencing, and categorizing—every KPI.

"What is this metric driving? Where does it belong?" I kept asking myself.

Finally, at the end of day three, a pattern emerged. Out of the 140 metrics, 12 kept showing up as anchors. Everything else rolled up under them. I could see a story emerging.

The next morning, I walked back into the CFO's office with one visual: 12 KPIs at the top, and 128 metrics cascading under them. A simple storyboard.

The CFO looked at the tree, then looked at me. She was very skeptical. But after one leadership meeting using only the 12 KPIs, she saw the difference. No "define the metric" debates. No scrolling through pages of KPIs. They focused on next steps to address some of the lagging KPIs.

Now the team had a daily pulse on the business—a single snapshot. With a glance, they could see what was off target and get to fixing it.

A few weeks later, I received an unexpected recommendation via email: "We were working with over 140 KPIs on numerous Excel spreadsheets. Through Mico's approach, we completed an interactive visual dashboard with 12 KPIs. By knowing what was tracking off target and taking corrective action, we were able to minimize risks and improve results."

I'm not sharing this to impress you. I was genuinely petrified walking into that room to tell a team of senior leaders that 91%—that's 128—of the KPIs they had been tracking for years were useless. Thank God the storyboard did the heavy lifting for me.

It removed emotion. It removed politics. It shifted the conversation from "defining metrics" to "deciding what to do next."

You'd think this would be an isolated case. It's not. Different industries, different countries, same pattern: monster KPI lists, meetings spent debating numbers, little to no action, and stalled decisions.

And this isn't limited to finance teams. Across sectors, executive scorecards routinely track dozens of metrics. Dashboards cram in 10 or more KPIs. Reports stretch to 30 or 40.

Studies show that your brain can actively process a maximum of four items at once. Research from George Miller and Nelson Cowan proves it: your brain maxes out at four chunks of information. Period.

It doesn't matter how smart or how senior you are—information overload stalls decisions for everyone.

Harvard Business Review calls this the "surrogation trap"—when organizations measure everything, they end up managing nothing. Science proves it. The business world ignores it.

This is exactly why 88% of insights never influence a single decision. This is where that $777 billion in data talent goes to waste—not in bad data, but in false alignment disguised as consensus.

But metric overload isn't a technology problem. It's an alignment problem.

Alignment breaks when leaders aren't unified on a single outcome. And when metrics aren't tied to that outcome, teams default to tracking everything—because cutting feels risky, and clarity feels political.

That's how KPI lists quietly grow to 50. . . 100. . . Even 140 metrics.

Metric overload isn't the real problem. It's a symptom.

The real issue is an alignment crisis—one that happens long before any dashboard, report, or slide deck is built.

And until it's addressed, data analytics projects will continue to deliver insights—without ever driving decisive action.

THE REAL ALIGNMENT CRISIS: FALSE CONSENSUS

If the telecom binder story sounds familiar, there's a reason.

Here's what I didn't understand back then: the problem wasn't that the leadership team disagreed; it's that they *thought* they agreed.

And that thinking, over the course of a decade, led to a physical binder with 140-plus metrics—and counting.

As I sat through a few of their meetings prior to getting handed the binder, I watched the binder grow in real time.

I attended a customer success meeting just to gain context, as someone said, "We really need to focus on customer retention."

Everyone nodded.

"And we should track churn," someone noted.

More nods.

"But we also need to understand acquisition cost."

Nods again.

"And what about lifetime value, engagement, and NPS?"

No one pushed back—disagreement feels like disloyalty. No one dug deeper—clarity feels political.

So everyone nodded and walked out feeling aligned. Everyone assumed they were building toward the same goal.

They were not.

Different movies were playing in each person's head.

And no one caught it because out loud all the metrics "made sense."

This is the crisis. This is exactly how 140 metrics are born.

Not from incompetence. Not from bad communication. From false alignment.

They were all prioritizing the "right metrics"—just for completely *different versions* of the goal.

False alignment is costly and dangerous.

Unlike misalignment—where people openly disagree—false alignment is invisible. You can't talk your way out of it—everyone thinks they agree. You can't analyze your way out of it—data won't reveal the different mental movies.

The false alignment crisis is not just costing companies. It's killing careers.

Data and business professionals who can't engineer alignment get stuck as order takers forever—building what's asked for instead of what's needed. In the age of AI, it's a death sentence. While AI handles the technical stuff, your value is your ability to drive human decisions. Be a decision driver. And you can't do that without alignment.

So how do you break false alignment?

You make the invisible visible. Force everyone to watch the same movie. Create one clear picture they can all see at once.

That's exactly why Hollywood directors don't pitch $200 million movies with words. They pitch with storyboards—visual blueprints that get every stakeholder watching the same story before a single frame is shot.

And it's exactly what you need to do. But here's what most people get wrong about storyboarding.

THE ART OF STORYBOARDING

Most professionals think storyboarding is just a process—something you use to organize information. They're wrong.

It's an art. The art of engineering alignment in a world that is drowning in insights.

And here's what nobody tells you: you can't engineer alignment by building something perfect and presenting it. You have to create it before you build anything.

I learned this the hard way.

For years, I used the storyboard as an information-gathering tool, not an alignment tool.

I'd walk into a conference room, write "Goal, Key Metrics, Insights, Actions" in a neat vertical row on the whiteboard, and then ask, "What's the goal?"

That was the only question we'd answer.

Everyone would start talking at once. I'd stand at the board trying to write each of their answers. We'd spend hours debating what "success" meant. If we got to the KPIs in the first session, we were lucky. In the end, the "loudest" or most "senior" person in the room always prevailed. So much for democracy.

Those UAT (user attack) sessions became like *Groundhog Day*.

I had the storyboard. I had the questions. What I didn't have was control of the process.

I had no idea how to slow things down. How to handle debates. How to create a safe space where every voice was heard.

Instead of helping them build their story, I was playing referee—managing noise, tiptoeing around egos, and giving "5 minutes left" reminders. Ugh.

I was so focused on getting information that I missed the most important part: the journey—creating an experience that produces alignment.

Scientists call it "inter-brain synchrony." I call it "getting everyone on the same page."

When teams collaborate well, their brain activity synchronizes. When used correctly, the storyboard creates that harmony. It turns scattered ideas into a clear decision pathway.

That's the art of storyboarding. It doesn't just capture a story; it captures a vision they actually want to own.

So how do you actually create that journey?

STEP 2: DEFINE—BUILDING THE STORY

You stop reacting to chaos. You start following a clear structure.

As shown in Figure 6.1, the Data Storytelling Storyboard has four parts. Four questions. One shared story.

But you don't build the story in one shot. You guide stakeholders through three focused sprints—each sprint designed to move the story forward.

- **Sprint 1:** Align the Vision
- **Sprint 2:** Validate the Plan
- **Sprint 3:** Commit to Action

Everything starts with Sprint 1. Without a shared definition of success, everything else is noise.

The key to using the storyboard and questions is to get alignment and buy-in. To do this, you can't just ask the questions and move on—you need

Figure 6.1   The Data Storyteller Storyboard

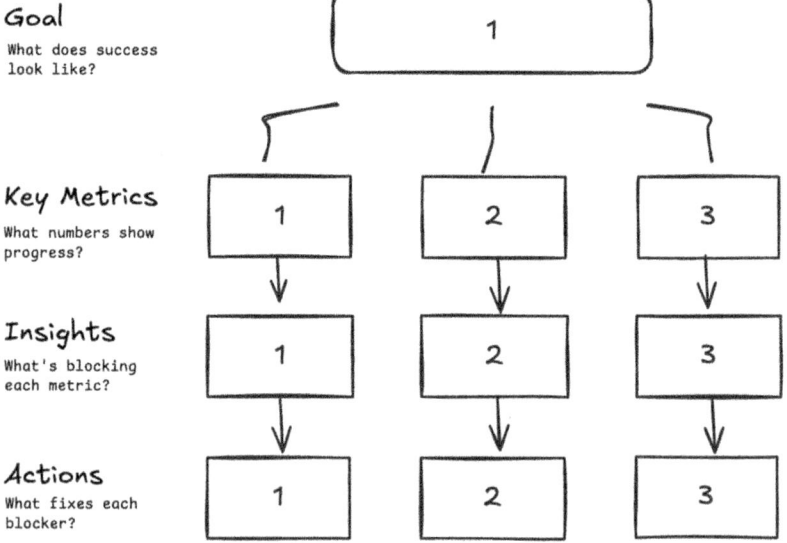

to ensure everyone is on the same page as you finalize the goal, each metric, insight, and action.

Research from Harvard, Yale, and Duke proves that when people create something, they value it five times more than if they did not create it—which is why letting your stakeholders define their metrics creates unstoppable buy-in.

Trust me, you want to own the data, but *not* the story. Big difference. So many people get this wrong and then wonder why the business doesn't trust them, why it feels like you're questioning their authority, why your recommendations get ignored, and why you only get credit when the numbers are wrong.

Let me show you how these three sprints work. But first, a quick note.

Before Sprint 1, you should handle the discovery questions (who, when, what) offline via email or DM. There's no need for an entire session—just get the basic context so you can focus Sprint 1 on the story.

THE THREE STORYBOARD SPRINTS

Sprint 1: Align the Vision (60–90 Minutes)

Alignment doesn't happen by accident.

Sprint 1 is your most critical session. In 90 minutes, you need to walk your stakeholders from "We think we know what we want" to "We see, agree, and know what we want."

Your goal: leave the room with a draft storyboard that includes the following:

- A single clear goal
- 3–5 key metrics
- A list of raw insights
- A short list of potential actions

If you get this right, everything else is just execution. If you miss here, scope creep becomes your friend.

Here's the tricky part: Sprint 1 is not the time to try to be the genius in the room. I know this is hard, and it takes discipline. But as my mom used to say, "God gave you two ears and one mouth for a reason." Time to be quiet and listen.

I know it feels wrong. You've got insights. You've got experience. You've got opinions about what they should be measuring.

But even if they say the wrong thing—and they will—do not correct them at this phase. That's what Sprint 2 is for.

> Your biggest enemy in Sprint 1 is your own expertise. The moment you correct your stakeholders, challenge their metrics, or suggest "better" KPIs—you just took ownership of the story. Now it's *your* story, not theirs. And when it fails? That's on you, too. Why? Because if you define it, you own it. Period.

If you jump in now, without knowing the full story, you become the person who challenges their expertise. They're the SMEs (subject matter experts). It's their story. Not yours. They may ask questions, but keep it brief; do not continue to "enlighten" them.

It takes discipline. It may feel wrong. But trust me, it's absolutely right. They will feel seen, heard, and understood.

And if they don't know what they want, you should not have moved on from the Discover step in Chapter 5.

The Setup

You need sticky notes, markers, and a whiteboard. That's it.

If you are conducting the session in person, have everyone sit or stand facing the board.

If you are conducting the session remotely, you can use Miro, FigJam, or any digital whiteboard. The same rules apply.

If you can do the session in person, do it. It will be easier to spot the Three Signs of Influence. If not, conducting the session remotely works just fine. Just watch out for the following red flags:

- **No clarity:** Silence in the chat
- **No buy-in:** Cameras off and the mute button on

Now here's the key to the process: the art.

The Rules of Engagement

These aren't suggestions. They're the difference between alignment and another wasted meeting.

1. **No hierarchy:** Everyone writes their answers on a sticky note first. Everyone speaks to explain what they wrote. No one dominates. All inputs count.
2. **Visual ownership:** Everyone gets a different color set of sticky notes. Everyone feels seen. Easy to track who said what.
3. **Conflict resolution:** Group similar responses together. Let the room vote on the outliers. The top choices win. Democracy, not dictatorship.
4. **The parking lot:** Great ideas that don't fit. File them under "Golden Nuggets" in a separate section. Everyone feels heard. The conversation moves forward.

How to Run the Sprint

Here's exactly how to walk your stakeholders through the storyboard.

Row 1: The Goal (20–25 Minutes)

Start with the most important question: "What does success look like in 90 days?"

Why does 90 days matter? It's specific enough to be actionable and far enough to be meaningful. "End of year" is too vague. "Next week" is too tactical. Ninety days—or whatever reasonable timeframe is needed to see change—works here, as long as it's specific.

Here's the process:

1. Everyone writes their answers on a sticky note. Silently. No discussion yet. (2 minutes)
2. One by one, each person reads their sticky note and places it on the board. They briefly explain what they meant and answer any questions.
3. Group similar goals together. You hope to see clusters form.
4. By default, the cluster with the most stickies becomes the goal—but confirm with the group that they're comfortable removing the other options, and let the room vote.
5. There can be only one goal per storyboard. Write it cleanly at the top of your storyboard.

Here's where false alignment usually rears its ugly head—and how to handle it. The chosen goal might be "improve customer satisfaction." Everyone nods. But what does it actually mean?

Push for specifics. Make them fill in the blanks:

$[Action][goal]$ from $[where\ we\ are]$ to $[where\ we're\ going]$ by $[when]$

For example: "Improve customer satisfaction from 72% to 85% by March 31."

What. From where. To where. By when. That's the goal.

Watch for the signs. You already know how to spot nods of clarity and the "we/us" language when someone is bought in.

If you're not seeing both, stop. You don't have alignment yet. You still have a room full of people watching different movies. Dig deeper before you move on.

One more thing: you're not looking for the Action sign here. Not yet. They're not committing to solve the business problem—they're committing to the story. We'll look for action in Chapter 7. For now, focus on Clarity and Buy-In.

Now reconfirm the Goal: "Does this goal make sense to everyone, or would we like to adjust anything?"

Look for the nods. Move on.

Row 2: Key Metrics (20–25 Minutes)

Now that you have the goal, your stakeholders need to know if they're winning.

Ask: "What 3–5 numbers would tell us we're on track to hit this goal?"

Not "all the KPIs we currently track." Three to five metrics that directly impact the goal they just defined.

This is where the 140-KPI crowd gets nervous. They want to track everything. Your job is to help them focus.

Follow the same process as the goal—write, share, group, prioritize. Three to five key metrics max. They know the drill.

Watch for the following:

- **Vanity metrics:** Ones that have no direct impact on the goal. Someone suggests "social media followers" when the goal is

reducing churn. Um, no. But you don't say that, remember? Politely redirect: "How does that tell us we're reducing churn?"
- **Metric overlap:** "Customer satisfaction" and "NPS" might be measuring the same thing. Cluster these.

Once you're done grouping and prioritizing, make sure each key metric follows the same format as the goal:

"[Action][Key Metric] from [where we are] to [where we're going] by [when]."

For example: "Reduce response time from 2.4 hours to under 2 hours by the end of Q1."

What we're measuring. Where we are. Where we're going. By when.

Check for clarity and buy-in after each key metric. If you're not seeing both, slow down before moving to Row 3.

To confirm, ask: "Are we good with these key metrics, or should we change something?" (Point to the key metrics.)

Row 3: Insights (15–20 Minutes)

The goal is set. The metrics are locked. Now: what's standing in the way?

Ask: "What's currently stopping us from hitting these numbers?" (Do this for one key metric at a time.)

Follow the same process as the goal—write, share, group, prioritize. But here's where it gets interesting.

When you ask, "what's blocking us," you're giving them permission to name the elephants in the room. The politics. The broken promises. The resource constraints everyone knows about but nobody says out loud. It's important to focus on insights you can actually confirm with data.

Not: "I think our team is not being productive enough." That's a management problem, not a data problem. But: "I think productivity is down due to constant system failures." That you can measure.

Watch for the following:

- **Symptoms vs. root cause:** Someone says, "We need more staff." That's a symptom. Dig deeper: "Why do you need more staff? What's driving the workload?" You might discover the real issue is, "We're handling the same customer issue 4 times because our knowledge base is outdated."
- **Blame games:** If insights turn into finger-pointing, redirect: "Let's focus on the process, not the people. What's the real issue here?"
- **The "we've always done it this way" blocker:** This is gold. When someone admits a legacy process is the problem, you've hit the insights gold mine.

Check for clarity and buy-in after grouping the insights: "Does everyone agree these are the real blockers?"

Look for nods, then move to Row 4.

Row 4: Actions (15–20 Minutes)

You have the Goal. You have the Key Metrics. You have their gut Insights. Now it's time to learn what they think they can do to fix the blockers.

Ask: "What specific actions could address these blockers?"

Again, use the same process—write, share, group, prioritize. But here's the critical difference: In Sprint 1, you're collecting ideas for actions. They still need to be validated.

Watch for the following:

- **Vague actions:** "Improve communication" means nothing. Push for specifics: "What would better communication look like? Who needs to communicate what to whom?"
- **Quick wins vs. big bets:** You want a mix. Just try to avoid boiling the ocean. Some actions should be "we can do this next week." Others might be "this is a 90-day project."

By the End of Sprint 1

By the end of Sprint 1, you should have:

- A clear goal (targets and timelines still need validation)
- 3–5 key metrics (targets and timelines still need validation)
- Insights showing what they think is blocking each metric (gut knowledge)
- A prioritized list of potential actions (ideas, not commitments)

This is the first draft of the storyboard.

Next step: validation.

Sprint 2: Validate the Plan (24–48 Hours)

Sprint 1 gave you your stakeholders' vision. Sprint 2 will test whether it's legit.

This is where your data superpowers finally get to shine. Now that you have their version of the story, your job is to validate it with data.

Sprint 2 isn't a session—it's your homework. You've been quiet. You've listened. You've let them define the story. Now it's time to do what you do best.

Plan for Sprint 3 to take place no more than 24–48 hours after Sprint 1—long enough to validate, short enough to keep momentum. Any longer and the energy dies. Worse, the answers start shifting.

Start pressure-testing every assumption they made as soon as you can.

Here's the reality: stakeholders lie to themselves all the time. Not on purpose. They genuinely believe their gut hunches are facts.

- "Our churn is around 15%." (Actually, it's 23%.)
- "Customers love the new feature." (Um, no. Usage dropped 40%.)
- "We're hitting our targets." (Are we? The data shows you haven't hit a single target in three quarters.)

Your job in Sprint 2 is not to prove them wrong. It's to prove the story is legit—or fix it before anything is built.

What to Watch For

Three things:

- **Confirmation:** Their gut hunches were right. The data backs it up. Check. Move forward.
- **Contradiction:** Their gut hunches were wrong. The data shows something completely different. Flag it and address it.
- **Gaps:** They missed something entirely. The data reveals a new problem nobody mentioned—a new insight.

Most storyboards have all three. Some things are confirmed. Some things are contradicted. Some things nobody saw coming.

This is all normal. That's why validating before building is key.

The Process

Take the storyboard from Sprint 1. Think of everything as a hypothesis until you validate it.

- **The Goal:** Is their 90-day target actually achievable, or is it fantasy dressed up as ambition?

    Pull the historical data. If they've never reduced churn by more than 2% in a quarter, a goal of an 8% reduction needs a conversation.
- **The Key Metrics:** Do the numbers they picked actually exist? Are their targets realistic? Are they measured consistently?

    You'd be shocked how often stakeholders confidently name metrics that don't exist—or metrics that have a different definition in every system.

- **The Insights:** Do their gut hunches match reality?

    They said, "Customers are leaving because of price." But your data shows 69% of churned customers cited support response time—not price.

- **The Actions:** Are their proposed fixes actually connected to the real problems?

    If the data says support response time is the issue, but their proposed action plan is "run a pricing study," you've got a gap.

The Validation Checklist

Before Sprint 3, you need answers to the following questions:

- **For the Goal**

☐ Is the target realistic based on historical performance?
☐ Is the timeline achievable?
☐ Do we have baseline data to measure against?

- **For each Key Metric**

☐ Does the metric exist, and is it accessible?
☐ Is it measured consistently across teams?
☐ What's the current baseline?

- **For each Insight**

☐ Does the data confirm or contradict their hypothesis?
☐ What's the actual evidence?
☐ Are there insights the data reveals that weren't mentioned?

- **For each Action**

☐ Is the action connected to a validated insight?
☐ Do we have evidence this type of action works?
☐ Is it a quick win?

- **Your value-add**
- ☐ What did the data reveal that they didn't mention (new insights)?
- ☐ Based on what you found, what else should they consider (recommended actions)?

The Updated Storyboard

You're walking into Sprint 3 with a refined version of their storyboard. Same structure. Validated story parts.

- **Where the data confirmed their hunches:** Note it. Put a check mark in the top-right corner of the sticky note, or change the sticky note color to green if you're working digitally.

    "Data validates: churn is 23%, driven primarily by support response time."

- **Where the data contradicts:** Flag it. Put a red or orange sticky note with a note over it, or add a comment to the sticky note if you're working digitally.

    "Data shows a different pattern: 68% cite support, only 12% cite price."

- **Where you find gaps:** Fill them. Put a red or orange sticky note with a note over it, or add a comment to the sticky note if you're working digitally. If it's a new insight, use a neutral color.

    "Additional insight from data: 40% of churned customers had 3+ support tickets in their final month."

You now have a storyboard that is validated and strengthened with evidence. No hallucinations. No gut analysis. True insights. True outputs.

The Mindset

Sprint 1 was about listening and guiding.

Sprint 2 is about analyzing and confirming. You validate the story.

In Sprint 1, you were the guide—listening, facilitating, staying neutral, and letting them define the story. In Sprint 2, you're the expert. You did the homework. You quantified their hunches. You found the patterns they couldn't see. And now you're coming back with proof.

It may be tempting, but do not skip this step. It's easy to jump straight to design after Sprint 1, when you got it from the "horse's mouth." But "I think" and "I feel" are not reality. They are hunches and gut feelings—still valid, but they can be a hallucination.

Your job is to keep everyone honest and give them insights and recommendations they can actually use to make decisions.

Now that you've done the homework, it's time to get sign-off.

Sprint 3: Commit to Action (60 Minutes)

Remember when I told you not to give your input in Sprint 1? Sprint 3 is the exact opposite.

This is where you build trust. You go from being seen as an order-taker to becoming a decision driver.

Sprint 3 is a 60-minute session. This time, you're not just guiding—you're providing data-driven insights and actions.

This is where the storyboard becomes real. Names get attached to actions. Deadlines get locked in.

Walking Back into the Room

Now that you're armed with facts and insights, it's important that you approach them correctly.

Not: "Actually, you all were wrong. The data shows. . ." Might as well say goodbye to buy-in.

Instead, start with something like: "I went back and validated everything we captured against the data. Most of it was solid. A few things looked different than we discussed. Let me walk you through my findings."

Big difference.

You're not saying they were wrong. You're letting the data shift the conversation.

When the Data Disagrees

This is the moment that separates traditional data storytellers from decision drivers.

Don't say: "You said churn was 15%, but you were wrong. It's actually 23%."

Say: "You estimated churn around 15%. The data shows 23%. What do you think is driving the gap?"

"The data shows something different" keeps the focus on the data. "You were wrong" points the finger at them.

One preserves psychological safety. One destroys it.

Remember: They defined it, so they own it. Your job is to refine it with evidence, not replace it with your version.

The Walkthrough

Go section by section. Same order as Sprint 1. Same Hollywood structure.

- **The Setup:**
  - **Goal:** "Here's the goal we agreed on. Based on historical data, here's why it's achievable—or here's what we might need to adjust."
  - **Metrics:** "These are the metrics we discussed. Here are the current baselines. This is what we're measuring against."

- **The Villain:**
  - **Insights:** "You said X was the problem. The data confirms it—here's the evidence." Or: "The data showed something different. Here's what it revealed."
- **The Resolution:**
  - **Actions:** "Based on validated insights, here are the actions that might make sense. Which ones sound correct?"

    Watch for Sign #1 (Clarity) and Sign #2 (Buy-In) the whole time.

    Are they nodding? Do they get it? Are they saying "we" and "our" instead of "you" and "your"? That's ownership forming in real time.

    If they start to ask, "When do we start this?" before you do—great. Let them run with it. But your focus here is to get sign-off, not pushing for immediate action.

Lock In the Commitment

This is where you drive accountability.

For every action on the storyboard, you need to add:

- **Who owns it:** Be sure to get a name—not a team. A person.
- **When it's due:** Be sure to get a date—not "soon," not "Q2." A specific date.
- **What "done" looks like:** Be sure to get clarity—not "work on documentation." "FAQ section rewritten and published with answers to the top 10 support questions by next Friday."

Say it out loud in the room.

"So Anna owns updating the knowledge base articles by Friday. Hunter owns the password-reset fix by next Wednesday. Charlotte owns the FAQ rewrite by the end of the month. Everyone aligned?"

Look for the nods.

If someone hesitates, address it now, not later.

"I'm sensing some hesitation. What's the concern?"

Get it on the table. Resolve it. Or adjust the commitment.

What You Leave With

One validated storyboard everyone agreed to:

- A goal with a clear action, target, and timeline
- 3–5 key metrics that directly impact the goal
- Insights showing what's blocking each key metric
- Actions with owners and deadlines attached

Here's the shift that just happened:

- In Sprint 1, you asked them to define the vision. (The Setup.)
- In Sprint 2, you validated it with evidence. (Confirmed the Villain.)
- In Sprint 3, you got explicit commitment. (Locked the Resolution.)

They defined it. You validated it. They own it.

It's not a storyboard anymore—it's a contract.

The Storyboard Contract

Before anyone leaves Sprint 3, confirm that you have:

☐ One goal with a target and a deadline

☐ Three to five key metrics with targets and deadlines

☐ Validated insights

☐ Actions with *who* and *when* outlined

If any box is unchecked, you don't have a contract—you have a wish list.

You just locked in commitment.

So why does this process work? It's not magic—it's science.

Let's dig into it.

WHY THE STORYBOARD WORKS

Here's something wild: when stakeholders build their story together, their brains literally synchronize. Neuroscientists call it *inter-brain synchrony*—and it predicts which teams succeed and which ones fail.

That's why co-creation beats note-taking every time. When you go off and build what *you* think they need, you're directing your own movie. When you guide them to build the story together, it's *their* story. Their brains sync up because they are watching the *same* movie they filmed together.

Here's why the sequence matters.

Goal → Key Metrics → Insights → Actions is not random. It mirrors how your brain processes group decisions.

The *Goal* activates the reward system in your brain. "What does success look like?"

The *Key Metrics* engage your analytical reasoning. "How do we know we're winning?"

The *Insights* trigger your problem-solving networks. "What's blocking us?"

The *Actions* activate your commitment mechanisms. "What do we do about it?"

If you start with key metrics before you have a set goal, or jump to insights with no goal or key metrics, your brain literally can't commit. It doesn't have enough context to know what it's truly committing to.

This is why Hollywood's three-act structure has worked for a century: Setup → Conflict → Resolution. Your brain is wired for it.

And here's why Sprint 2 is a game-changer for us data folks.

According to research on building trust, when you consistently provide stakeholders with insights they couldn't get elsewhere, their brains start making "calculated predictions" that you're reliable, dependable, and professional.

- **Sprint 1:** You listened carefully. You let them define.
- **Sprint 2:** You did the homework and validated. You found things they missed.
- **Sprint 3:** You delivered insights that proved the story—or refined it with evidence.

By the time you walk into Sprint 3, their guard is down. They're open to your ideas—not just because of your title or experience, but because you used data to guide them, not your opinions.

This is not soft skills. It's neuroscience applied to influence.

Before you run off and go storyboard-crazy on every project, however, here's when *not* to use it.

WHEN TO USE THE STORYBOARD (AND WHEN TO SKIP IT)

The storyboard isn't for everything.

For the context of this book, we are focused on using it to create three kinds of data visualizations—dashboards, reports, and slide decks.

Use the storyboard when:

- Multiple stakeholders need to agree on what success looks like
- Someone has to *act* on your insights, not just see them
- The request is ambiguous, and you're not about to waste weeks building the wrong thing
- You're spending more than a few hours on something

Skip it when:

- It's a factual question with one right answer
- It's a routine report you're just refreshing
- It has one stakeholder and a crystal-clear ask—no ambiguity
- It's a 30-minute task, not a multi-week project

The filter is simple: If the outcome depends on other people acting and you're about to invest real time—do a storyboard first. It takes 90 minutes but can save weeks of back-and-forth.

If it's routine, operational, or ad hoc in nature, then skip it.

In some cases, you may even stop at this step. Not every storyboard needs to become a dashboard. Sometimes the alignment *is* the deliverable. Teams walk out with a shared goal, clear metrics, and committed actions—no visualization required.

But whether you build a dashboard or not, the storyboard process itself is a skill. And like any skill, you need to practice it.

Your Assignment Before Chapter 7

Here's what I want you to do before you move on:

Think about a project you are working on or have worked on in the past. Maybe it's a dashboard request from last week or a report that keeps getting revised. It could even be a presentation where you're not quite sure what to cover.

Pull up the dashboard, report, or slide deck.

Now draw a small storyboard and ask yourself these questions:

- What's the one goal?
- What 3–5 key metrics tell us we're winning?
- What's currently blocking those key metrics?
- What actions could address those blockers?

If you can answer all of them clearly, you're set.

If you can't, chances are alignment is missing or you have false consensus. The math ain't mathing. It's time to go back to the drawing board.

The storyboard just did a quick gap analysis for you. You should be able to instantly spot gaps in the story and their alignment.

When you're actually ready to run your first real storyboard session, start with a low-stakes project. Don't be like me in New York. Ugh. Work with a team you feel comfortable with and tell them you're trying a new process to really ensure you understand their story. Do this at least three times—then you're ready for the big leagues.

Remember: you're not just gathering requirements.

You're engineering alignment.

You're becoming known as a decision driver.

You now have alignment. You have a validated story. You have ownership. Now it's time to bring the story to life.

Chapter 7 shows you how to use your storyboard to design visuals that work with your stakeholders' brains, not against it. They drive decisions, not analysis paralysis.

CHAPTER SEVEN

DESIGN— VISUALS THAT DRIVE ACTION

"Any intelligent fool can make things bigger and more complex. It takes a touch of genius to move in the opposite direction."
—E.F. Schumacher

The phone rang at 9:30 a.m. on a Friday morning. Never good news.

"Mico, I need to talk to you about the dashboard."

My stomach sank. Oh no. I knew that tone.

It was the VP of Customer Success I'd been working with. Three weeks earlier, we had done a storyboard session with his team, and he was thrilled.

"This looks great. Happy to see the team on the same page," he'd said, looking at the storyboard.

That was three weeks ago.

Now?

"The storyboard was perfect," he continued as his voice dropped. "Everyone bought in. But when I showed them the dashboard. . ."

Long pause.

"They looked overwhelmed and confused. Dina, our senior analyst, raised her hand and asked. . ."

He didn't even need to finish. I already knew.

"Is there a way to export this to Excel?"

Ugh. The dreaded export request. The kiss of death for any analytics project. It means the dashboard just became a glorified export tool. Months of work reduced to a single CSV file.

I wanted to crawl under my desk and hide.

"I think they asked to export to Excel to build out another report. This is exactly what I wanted to avoid. . ." he said with disappointment.

Export to Excel isn't a feature request. It's a sign of failure.

The storyboard had created alignment—but the dashboard was clearly broken. It had too much information crammed on one screen. Their brains shut down.

The alignment was still there. The design of the dashboard buried it.

I hate to admit it, but this wasn't the first time I'd gotten this feedback. It wasn't even the tenth time.

Our dashboards were landing in the digital graveyard—whether I'd like to admit it or not.

As if things couldn't get any worse, the following Monday, I was sitting at my desk, hot cup of green tea in hand.

A Gartner report email landed in my inbox.

"75% of analytics created are never used."

Three in four?

This had to be a joke, right?

Why do all this work if no one was going to use it?

The math wasn't mathing—and I had to know why.

WHY MOST DASHBOARDS DIE

Why were analytics, especially dashboards, going to the digital trash?

I had a front-row seat to something most researchers don't get—thousands of students and customers across global brands.

I wanted to see if the 75% was true.

My data scientist brain kicked into high gear.

I asked my team to run 30–60–90-day check-in calls with a few of our enterprise customers. Not just asking users how they felt, but actually looking at the usage stats over time.

What we found with our customers was way worse than Gartner.

A whopping 85–93% of dashboards were abandoned.

The 30–60–90-day analytics death spiral was everywhere.

And it was expensive. Every abandoned dashboard represented wasted development time, wasted licenses, and wasted server space.

It cost companies $420 billion annually.

That's not a typo. Four. Hundred. Twenty. Billion. Dollars.

Just crazy.

After we confirmed the death spiral was real, one question haunted me: why?

These weren't ugly dashboards. They weren't built by amateurs.

I pulled back up the VP's Customer Success storyboard and dashboard.

Storyboard: one goal, five key metrics, five insights, three actions.

Clean. Focused. Clear priorities.

The dashboard: same information.

So what went wrong?

It wasn't the design. It was the layout.

We tried to cram everything onto one page. Buried the goal at the top. Metrics scattered across the middle. Insights mixed with actions at the bottom.

What seemed aesthetically pleasing was actually quite overwhelming.

It was a pretty mess.

We were triggering analysis paralysis and cognitive overload.

Decisions can't be made in either state. The brain shuts down.

Time to go back to the drawing board.

Do we remove some of the data? Do we change the order of information?

Staring at the two screens later that night, I could see that we designed for the data. Showing a trend because they might want to see the history. A donut chart because they might want to see the breakdown. It was about making the data fit, not making a decision.

THE ANATOMY OF A DECISION TILE

Over the next few months, I dissected thousands of data visualizations. Dashboards that drove decisions. Dashboards that didn't. Slide decks that moved stakeholders. Slide decks that put them to sleep.

I was hunting for an answer. A pattern. A reason.

Here's what I discovered: The dashboards that actually drove a decision weren't necessarily well designed—they were just structured differently. They followed a pattern. A specific anatomy that works with how our brains process information to make a decision.

It turns out, I wasn't the first person to crack this code.

The U.S. military figured this out over 80 years ago.

August 1940, in London.

As bombs fall. Nazi Germany sits 21 miles across the English Channel. Britain stands alone.

Winston Churchill has just become Prime Minister. And every day he receives thick briefs on his desk—military intelligence, supply updates, strategic analysis. Pages and pages of reports.

Churchill had had enough.

In the middle of fighting a world war, he paused to write a one-page memo to his entire war cabinet.

Title: "BREVITY."

His complaint was blunt:

"To do our work, we all have to read a mass of papers. Nearly all of them are far too long. This wastes time, while energy has to be spent in looking for essential points."

Translation: He needed to make quick, strategic decisions and was drowning in information.

His solution was simple.

"Reports which set out the main points in a series of short, crisp paragraphs."

Short. Crisp. Main points first.

Churchill wasn't asking for prettier reports. He wasn't asking for simpler data. He was demanding that his commanders structure information for decisions—not for completeness.

Today the U.S. military calls this principle BLUF—Bottom Line Up Front. It's now official Army doctrine, codified in a 100-page regulation on effective writing. The regulation states that "the greatest weakness in ineffective writing is that it doesn't quickly transmit a focused message."

BLUF works because it mirrors how the brain triages information under pressure.

Churchill understood something fundamental: when stakes are high and time is short, structure beats volume.

Churchill was solving the same problem in 1940 that was plaguing our data industry 80 years later. Too much data. Too little insight. No decisions.

The questions weren't "What data should we show?" or "What charts should we use?" The question was "How do we structure information so our brains can actually make a decision?"

So I went back to all those dashboards I'd dissected—the ones that worked—and reverse engineered the pattern. What emerged was a repeatable structure I now call *Decision Tiles*.

Decision Tiles are designed for one purpose—to accelerate the decision.

They are self-contained blocks that answer one question completely. No hunting. No scrolling. No "let me export to Excel to find out."

Every Decision Tile follows the same anatomy—answering three questions:

- **What is happening:** The status of the key metric, immediately. Red, yellow, green. Easy to see if you're winning or losing.
- **Why it matters:** The key metric with context. Not just the number—the target. The insight that is driving the gap.
- **What to do about it:** The action. Written clearly with an owner and deadline.

Status. Key Metric. Insight. Action.

Three sections. One tile. One decision.

That is the anatomy of a Decision Tile.

Now let's build.

STEP 3: DESIGN VISUALS THAT DRIVE ACTION

You're the architect now.

You've got the story. You need the structure. You need to build something people will actually use.

Here's the challenge: Your storyboard has 16 pieces of critical information. One goal. Five key metrics. Five insights. Five actions. All essential. All fighting for attention.

But our brains can only process four chunks of information at a time. So, here's the rule: One dashboard. Four tiles. That's it.

THE 4-TILE STRUCTURE

Think of your dashboard as having two simple rows with four tiles (Figure 7.1).

I know that four tiles may feel restrictive. Uncomfortable. Even risky.

"What about all my other key metrics?"

"What if we need more detail?"

"What if my boss wants to see everything?"

Figure 7.1   The complete dashboard layout

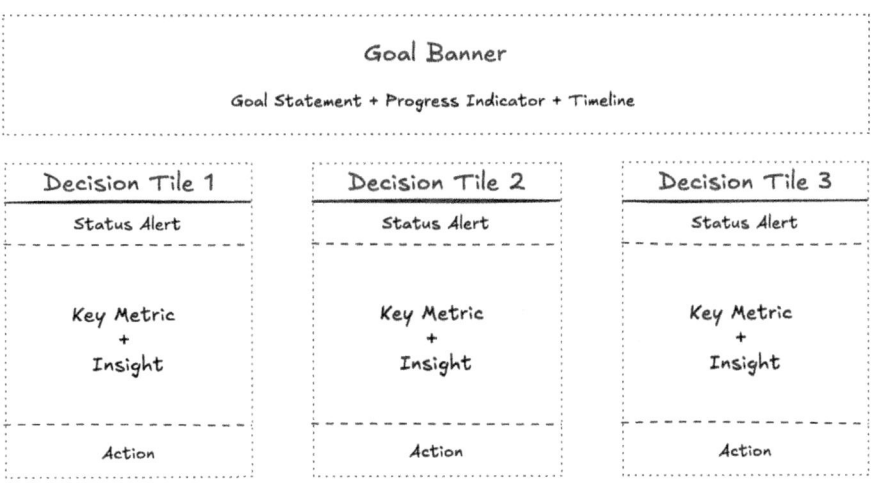

I hear you. It's tempting to want to continue to add data, but every additional piece of information distracts from the decision.

These constraints are not limitations—they're design intelligence.

The moment you remove the option to show everything, you're forced to show only what matters. And showing only what matters is exactly what drives decisions.

Let me walk you through each tile.

Row 1: The Goal Banner

The Goal Banner goes across the top row—taking up roughly 20% of the screen height.

This is not an addition; it's a replacement.

Most dashboards waste prime real estate on a generic title like "Customer Success Dashboard" or "Q3 Sales Report." Those are file names, not directions.

The Goal Banner takes that same space and gives it a job. Instead of labeling what they're looking at, you're telling them what they're working toward.

A goal like "Reduce support tickets from 1,200 to 800 per week" is a mission.

Why the top? Because that's where eyes go first.

Your eyes don't randomly wander—they follow a predictable pattern: top left, across, then down. It's called the F-pattern, and it's why burying the goal is the beginning of the end for any dashboard.

The first thing stakeholders see needs to answer the first questions in their head: *Why am I looking at this?*

The Goal Banner answers immediately.

It says, "Here's what we're trying to accomplish."

Everything below supports this.

The Goal Banner contains three elements:

- **Goal statement:** Pulled directly from your storyboard in Chapter 6. Write in plain language. "Trim overdue invoice by 40% in Q3."
- **Progress indicator:** Where are you versus where you need to be. A simple visualization showing the gap. "Currently at 12%. Target is 40%."
- **Timeline:** How much time is left. Deadlines create urgency. "6 weeks remaining."

That's it. No trend charts. No line graphs.

Just: Where are we going? How far along are we? How much time do we have?

The Goal Banner is your stakeholder's North Star. The other tiles on the dashboard exist to support it.

Common Goal Banner Mistakes

- **Keeping the generic dashboard title:** Your template doesn't need a separate title field. The Goal Banner *is* the title. Don't waste screen space with "Customer Success Dashboard" above the Goal Banner. That's just a file name, not a direction.
- **Making progress too complicated:** A simple progress bar showing current versus target beats a full trend chart every time. Your stakeholders need to know the gap in two seconds, not twenty. A sparkline showing trajectory? Fine. A 12-month historical breakdown? This just stops the flow and can trigger analysis too early.
- **Scattering the elements:** The goal statement, progress indicator, and timeline should stack vertically in the Goal Banner. Top to bottom. Don't spread them left to right across the banner. Keep the flow simple. Where we're going → Where we are → How much time is left.

Row 2: Three Decision Tiles

Below the Goal Banner, the remaining 80% of your screen has three tiles side by side—equal width, equal height.

One Decision Tile for each of your top three key metrics.

Your storyboard has five key metrics. You need to choose three. I'll cover how to do that next.

Each Decision Tile follows the anatomy you just learned (Figure 7.2).

Figure 7.2   Anatomy of a Decision Tile example

For each of your three key metrics, pull the matching insight and action from your storyboard:

- **Top (what is happening):** Status alert + key metric name
  - An indicator showing if you're winning—status colors red, yellow, or green.
  - The key metric name right next to it
- **Middle (why it matters):** The key metric
  - Big number (current value)
  - Target below it

- Simple visual to show the gap between (bullet chart or similar)
  - Insight in italics explaining "why"
- **Bottom (what to do next):** The action
  - What needs to happen
  - Who owns it
  - When it's due

One tile. One key metric. One complete decision story.

This structure puts everything a decision-maker needs in one place—in one view—making it easy to make a decision.

How to Select Your Three Key Metrics

Go back to your storyboard. You have five key metrics, five insights, and five actions.

Your dashboard fits three.

"But I have five key metrics. How do I prioritize?"

Simple.

By impact.

Which three key metrics have the biggest impact on the goal?

Ask: *If my stakeholders could only act on three things today, which three would move the goal fastest?*

That's the filter. Not what easiest to do. What drives the goal.

The other two metrics go to the appendix or a secondary view, not on the dashboard. Put them in a drill-down. A linked report. Not competing for attention.

Remember: As a decision driver, you don't ask, "What data should I show?" You ask, "What decision should this enable?"

Common Decision Tile Mistakes

- **Cramming two metrics into one tile:** You want one decision per tile. That's it. Adding an additional metric, insight, or action creates confusion. Split it into two tiles or cut one.

- **Including too much text:** Keep the key metric name short. Use just the name. For the insight, you want to stick to 5–6 words max. Make sure it's clear and tied back to how it impacts the key metric.

    Instead of this: "Current staffing gap is the main reason driving delays."

    Use this: "Staffing gap causing 40% of delays."

    One line. Driver + impact.

- **Making tiles different sizes:** They need to be equal width and height. This is nonnegotiable. When tiles are different sizes, the brain wastes energy trying to figure out what's important instead of processing the information. Keep it consistent.

The One-Screen Rule

Fitting your dashboard on a single screen is nonnegotiable.

No scrolling. Up or down.

Scrolling is usually the symptom of an incomplete storyboard.

When the story is clear, one screen is enough. When it's not, no amount of scrolling will help.

The dashboard should provide answers, not create questions.

If your dashboard generates questions—"What does this chart mean?" or "Where do I look first?"—it's creating noise.

A decision-focused dashboard answers four things instantly:

- Where are we going? (Goal Banner)
- What's happening with priority 1? (tile 1)
- What's happening with priority 2? (tile 2)
- What's happening with priority 3? (tile 3)

No hunting. No interpreting.

Here's something to remember: Every chart you add is a tax on your stakeholders' attention. Every filter is a decision they have to make before they can make the real decision. Every scroll is a chance for them to overanalyze.

The one-screen rule is design safety. It protects their mental space and enhances their decision-making.

From Storyboard to Slide Deck

Use the same structure. Different format.

Everything you learned about the dashboard structure applies to slides. The brain science doesn't change, but there are a few design changes.

- **Slide 1—Goal Banner:** Your goal statement, progress indicator, and timeline. Same content as the dashboard—with room for a bit more context (if needed).
- **Slide 2—Decision Tile 1:** Status alert + key metric + action. One complete decision story.
- **Slides 3–4: Same as Decision Tile 1**, but focused on the second and third key metrics.

Keep it simple. You can speak to the slides. Keep the message crisp and clear.

There are three major differences between a dashboard and slides:

Headlines Tell the Story

Each slide title is your status alert. Not "Q3 Revenue Metrics" but "Revenue is 12% below target—three accounts are driving the gap."

Your title should pass the "so what" test. If someone reads only the headline and skips everything else, do they know what's happening and why it matters?

Bad: "Customer Satisfaction Update"

Good: "Satisfaction dropped 15%—caused by billing errors"

The headline does the heavy lifting. Everything else on the slide supports it.

More Text Is Allowed

Dashboards are for scanning. Slides are for reading. You can add a sentence or two of context, but keep it short and simple.

Dashboards provide context with a short blurb of the insight. Slides expand on the insight a bit more and say, "Here's why this matters."

Keep it to two sentences max. Speak to the slides to provide more details.

You Control the Pace

In a dashboard, everything is visible at once. Your stakeholders' eyes can jump ahead to the decision. With slides, you control the pace. You can walk them through one decision at a time.

You want to speak to the slides but not lose momentum. Make sure your stakeholders are locked in (something I'll discuss in Chapter 8) before moving to the next slide.

This is your superpower as a presenter. Use it.

Don't rush through all four slides in five minutes. Walk your stakeholders through the Goal Banner first. Make sure they understand where you're going. Then reveal Decision Tile 1. Let them absorb it. Watch for the Three Signs (I'll cover this in Chapter 8.) Only move to the next slide when you see clarity and buy-in.

In a dashboard, your stakeholders control the pace. With slides, you do.

Common Slide Deck Mistakes

- **Copying the dashboard onto a slide:** Unless it's for a design review, do not simply cut and paste the dashboard into your slide deck. Dashboards are for self-service; slides are for presenting. As discussed previously, you want to present small chunks of information on each slide and take your audience through the story.
- **Reading the slide out loud:** The moment you read word-for-word, you lose your stakeholders. They read faster than you talk. They end

up annoyed and three sentences ahead of you. Your job is to add context, not narrate. The slides show the "what." You explain the "so what."

What about reports?

Same structure. Goal, then each key metric with its insight and action as sections. This chapter focuses mostly on dashboards and slides because that is where you can actually see decisions happen live.

WHY THIS WORKS

As the saying goes, "A picture is worth a thousand words."

I was about to find out just how many words on a hot summer day in the Middle East.

After weeks of meetings with the head of operations for a large multinational company, my team was determined to solve their problem. The company was very profitable—but was facing a huge cash flow crisis.

Overdue invoices were piling up. The net-180-day log was three times the size of the net-30. They were all listed in a 20-tab spreadsheet. (I feel exhausted even remembering it.)

Nobody knew which invoices to focus on.

The staff was fairly traditional. They had never really seen a dashboard before. They were threading through that spreadsheet, guessing which invoices to work on.

The head of operations was under pressure from the CFO. He challenged us to find a way to make sure the collections team was always working on the most "important" invoices each day—not just the "low hanging fruit."

Given the challenge, we did something that made everyone uncomfortable.

We reserved the biggest boardroom in the building. Massive round table. Theater-sized screen. Fully equipped audio room above. The works.

I asked the head of operations and the other stakeholders to go up to the audio room where no one could see them—and watch quietly. I then pulled a random collections team member—let's call him Joshua—and brought him into the room. The dashboard was displayed on the big screen.

Joshua walked in visibly nervous—a 50-foot screen towering above him. I could see the fear in his eyes. The overwhelm. This man had never seen a dashboard in his life, and now he was staring at one the size of a movie screen.

I stood up and smiled. "Joshua, thanks for your time. There's nothing to be nervous about. There is no right or wrong answer. We are just testing something."

He took a deep breath.

"Based on what you see on the screen, what do you think you're supposed to do?" I asked.

Then I hit my timer.

Ten seconds . . . nothing. His eyes were fixed on the screen.

Thirty seconds . . . still scanning. I could hear his heart pounding.

Forty-five seconds . . . nothing.

And then—

Joshua started to change.

His shoulders dropped. He wasn't confused anymore.

His eyes locked onto one section of the screen.

He leaned forward, pointing a finger at the screen with confidence.

About 90 seconds later, he looked to the side at me and said, "I need to focus on these two invoices?"

From my peripheral vision, I could see the executives in the audio room shaking each other's hands.

Keeping a straight face, I asked, "How do you know that?"

"These two are red. And they're in the net-180-plus buckets. I need to focus on those first."

"Am I correct?," he asked.

"Yes, that's exactly what we were hoping for. Thank you, Joshua."

Joshua went from being overwhelmed to deciding which invoices to focus on.

Here's the thing: Joshua didn't guess. He didn't ask for help. He didn't say "I think maybe these two?"

He said, "I need to focus on these two."

He had clarity. And that clarity gave him confidence.

The dashboard structure did the heavy lifting.

Joshua's dashboard looked like nothing I'd been taught about visual design—no fancy charts, no trend icons.

It had two things: a Goal Banner across the top and one single Decision Tile below. That's it.

And it worked.

We put the brain science to the test.

We're wired to scan information-heavy displays in a predictable F-pattern—top first, then down the left, then across.

That's exactly how Netflix designs their homepage. They've spent over $1 billion annually perfecting this science. Safe to say they know what they're doing.

When Joshua eyes hit the Goal Banner at the top—"Collect $500M of the $1.5B overdue invoices by December 31"—something shifted. You could see it in his face. His brain stopped hunting and locked onto solid ground:

"Okay, I know why I'm here."

Subconsciously, Joshua's brain started to sort everything on the dashboard into two buckets: "helps the goal" or "hurts the goal."

Next, his eyes dropped to the left. The Decision Tile below.

He saw just one number: $89 million. The largest overdue invoice. Big red text.

His brain didn't need instructions. It started asking the right questions automatically: How does this metric help me hit the goal? What's blocking me? What should I do?

The answers were all in row 2. No hunting. No scrolling.

The moment he saw that big red number, it was like a lightbulb went off: "There's my biggest opportunity. If I can just collect this *one* invoice, I'll be almost 18% toward the $500 million goal."

Bingo. He got it.

No stacked bar charts to show him the overdue buckets. No donut charts to show him the mix of invoices. No noise. Just a single number ("$89 million"), simple text ("overdue 108 days"), and a progress bar to show the 18% progress he could make.

He was locked into collecting the $89 million invoice to put a dent in the goal.

One thing became crystal clear: everything we knew about dashboard design was completely backward.

For years, I'd been designing dashboards based on who would use them.

"This is for executives, so make it high-level."

"This is for analysts, so add more detail."

"This is for operations staff, so keep it simple."

All wrong.

Joshua understood what to do—not because we designed it for the "operations staff."

We designed it for decision-making. The task, not the person.

Research shows it doesn't matter if you're the CEO or a collections worker—your brain scans the same way, overwhelms the same way, and shuts down the same way when there's too much.

I wasn't teaching design anymore. I was teaching people how to work with the brain, not against it.

Good design creates clarity. Clarity creates buy-in. Buy-in creates action.

Here's what made that moment in the boardroom so significant: Joshua didn't just understand the dashboard; he owned the decision. He didn't say, "I think maybe I should focus on these?" He said, "I need to focus on these two." Declarative. Certain. Confident.

That shift—from tentative interpreter to confident decision-maker—is what we're designing for.

Traditional dashboards create information consumers—people who look at data and say, "Interesting, I'll need to think about this."

Decision Tile dashboards create action-takers—people who look at the data and say, "I know exactly what to do next."

That's not design preference; it's a fundamental difference in outcome.

And it happens not because Decision Tile dashboards have better data—Joshua had the same critical information that lived in those 20-tab spreadsheets. It happens because the structure matches how brains actually decide.

Structure beats volume every time.

Joshua proved that in 90 seconds.

If Joshua, who had never seen a dashboard before, could make the right call that fast—the only thing standing between your stakeholders and fast decisions is the correct structure.

But we weren't done. One test wasn't enough. We needed to know if it would hold.

Over the next two weeks, we ran the same test with six more collections team members. Same setup. Same questions. Same timer.

The results were consistent. Some got 60 seconds. Others took the full 90. But every single person could tell us what to do—without asking for help, without reaching for Excel.

We tweaked the design based on their feedback, adjusting the wording and simplifying the status colors—small refinements.

WHEN DESIGN GOES WRONG

I know what you're thinking: This is too simple. Where are all the charts? My stakeholders expect more visualizations.

I can see you now, leaning back with your arms crossed and eyebrows raised.

Trust me. I get it. That was my exact reaction before I put Joshua's dashboard on that 50-foot screen. I knew it looked nothing like a traditional dashboard.

For years, I thought dashboards meant charts. Reports meant text. Slide decks meant bullet points.

I was wrong.

Complexity often masquerades as credibility.

The more charts we show, the safer we feel. This safety often creates analysis paralysis for the end user.

And here's the thing: every data book teaches the same stuff—how to make better charts, tell better stories, get more engagement.

Nobody teaches how to design for speed to action.

Netflix has thousands of movies and shows. They could show you everything on the front page. Every genre. Every category. Every title.

They don't say, "Here are 47 shows you might like." Instead, they say, "Because you watched *The Chosen*, watch *House of David*."

One movie recommendation. Top of your screen.

Fast decision.

That's not dumbing down. That's a billion dollars of research proving simplicity wins.

The same brain science applies to your dashboards.

So where do most traditional dashboards go wrong?

Four places.

First: Cramming too much on the screen. Trying to visualize every metric. Every trend. Every data point somebody might want to see.

Impressive to look at. Impossible to act on.

Meanwhile, the goal is nowhere in sight. The actions never made it onto the screen. Just charts, trends, and status alerts.

Here's a rule of thumb: if your dashboard requires any form of "training" or "PDF guide," it's too hard.

Time to go back to the storyboard. Start at the top. Stick to the 4-tile dashboard structure.

Second: Burying the goal. . .or skipping it entirely.

Most dashboards don't display the goal. Users land on the screen, and aside from the dashboard title "Customer Churn Dashboard," they have no idea why they're there. They're expected to figure out what matters, why its matters, and what to do next.

Here's another rule of thumb: if someone can't tell you the goal within five seconds of looking at your dashboard, everything else becomes noise.

Put the Goal Banner at the top. Always.

Third: No clear actions. You show everything that happened, but nothing about how to actually fix it—the classic rearview-mirror dashboard.

Users see the problem, but they don't see the path forward. So they export to Excel to figure it out themselves.

The last rule of thumb: if your dashboard shows the "what" but not the "now what," you've built a report, not a decision tool.

That's why actions are clearly written at the bottom of every Decision Tile.

Fourth. Over-designing for aesthetics. Your dashboard isn't art; it's a decision tool.

That means no gradient fills because they "look cool." No custom fonts that match your personal style. No extra charts added just to fill white space.

Every visual element should have a job. If it's not helping your stakeholders make a decision faster, it's slowing them down.

Stick to the template. Use brand colors where required, bold for action, and italics for insights. That's it.

The goal isn't to win a design award. It's to get them from confusion to clarity in 90 seconds.

Pretty doesn't drive decisions. Clarity does.

YOUR TURN

Now that you know the structure and have seen the proof, it's your turn to build.

Let's convert the storyboard from Chapter 6 into a 4-tile dashboard.

Grab a piece of paper and a pencil. This is a mockup—not a finished product.

We're starting small. Just two tiles: the Goal Banner and one Decision Tile.

If you have gaps for actions or other data points, just fill in placeholder values. The goal is to understand the design structure, not to perfect the data.

Step 1: Build the Goal Banner

Figure 7.3 shows the basic structure of a Goal Banner. It contains three elements:

- **Goal statement**: Pull it directly from your storyboard. For example: "Boost profitability by $70M by Q4."
- **Progress indicator**: Place it below the goal statement. Show where you are versus where you need to be. "Currently at $21M (30% of the goal)."
- **Timeline**: Position it at the bottom. Show how much time is left. "Six weeks remaining."

Notice the flow:

1. The goal tells you where you're going ($70M profitability).
2. The progress indicator shows where you are ($21M/30%).
3. The visual shows the gap at a glance.
4. The timeline tells you how much time is left (six weeks).

Again, the Goal Banner is the North Star. Everything below it ladders up to this. No goal = no clarity. No clarity = no buy-in = no decision.

Figure 7.3   Goal Banner example

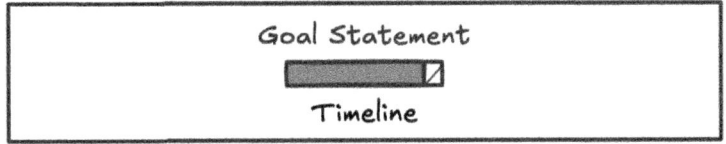

Step 2: Build the First Decision Tile

Figure 7.4 shows an example of a completed Decision Tile. Follow these steps to sketch your own.

Figure 7.4 Decision Tile example

Pick the most important key metric from your storyboard—the one that has the highest impact on the goal. The one that moves the needle.

Sketch it out.

- **Top: Status + key metric name**
  - Draw a filled circle (●) to indicate it's off track.
  - Write the key metric name next to it. Example: "Gross Margin"

- **Middle: Key metric number + insight**
  - Write the current value large and bold. Example: "**28%**"
  - Write the target smaller below it. Example: "Target: 32%"
  - Draw a simple bar: solid = achieved, empty = remaining
  - Below the bar, write the insight in *italics*—the "why" behind the gap. Example: *"Expedited shipping eating 40% of margin loss"*
- **Bottom: Action**
  - Write the action in bold—what to do, who owns it, and when it's due. Example: "**Shift default to standard shipping (Ops—Feb 15)**"

Notice the decision flow:

1. The status tells you there's a problem.
2. The key metric number shows where you are (28%).
3. The target shows where you need to be (32%).
4. The visual shows the gap.
5. The insight explains why (expedited shipping costs).
6. The action tells you exactly what to do (change shipping default, ops owns it, due by Feb 15).

A decision-maker can look at this tile, understand the full picture, and make a confident decision whether to act—in seconds. No need to export to Excel.

Step 3: Build the Second and Third Decision Tiles

You've nailed the first Decision Tile. Now repeat the process for the next two key metrics.

Decision Tile 2:

Pick your second-highest-impact metric from the storyboard.

- **Top: Status + key metric name**
  - Draw filled circle (●) to indicate it's off track
  - Write the key metric name next to it. Example: "Operating Cost"
- **Middle: Key metric number + insight**
  - Write the current value large and bold. Example: "**$48M**"
  - Write the target smaller below it. Example: "Target: $42M"
  - Draw a simple bar: solid = achieved, empty = remaining
  - Below the bar, write the insight in italics—the "why" behind the gap. Example: *"Overtime labor driving 55% of cost overrun"*
- **Bottom: Action**
  - Write the action in bold—what to do who owns it, and when it's due. Example: **"Cap overtime at 10 hrs/wk (HR—Feb 28)"**

The third Decision Tile follows the exact same structure. Repeat the preceding steps for your third highest-impact metric.

Step 4: Test It

This is the most important step. Don't skip it.

It's time to put the rubber to the road. Find someone who is unfamiliar with your work. Show them your paper mockup and ask: "Based on what you see, what do you think you're supposed to do?"

If they can answer you in 90 seconds or less, you nailed it. You just built a Decision Tile that works.

If they hesitate or ask for clarification, go back and simplify. Look at your wording. Less is more. No shame. Joshua's dashboard went through many iterations that night to get every single detail right. Self-editing is hard.

If you get asked questions like "Where's all the detail?," add that information in a drill-down, in an appendix, or in the linked report. The dashboard is for decisions, not exploration. Detail is one click away for those who need it.

"Can we add one more metric?" Sure—let's reopen the storyboard and revisit all of our metrics to ensure they are aligned with the goal and a top priority.

"This seems too simple." Good. Simple means they'll actually use it. Complex means export to Excel.

Here's my rule of thumb: anything that takes more than 90 seconds to understand is too confusing. Period. Cut until it works.

Within 90 seconds, your test subject should be able to tell you:

- What the goal is
- Whether we're winning or losing
- What they should do next

If they can do all three without asking questions, you built a decision tool.

If they reach for a filter, ask for context, or mention Excel—back to Step 3.

READY TO DELIVER

Congratulations! You've done the homework.

In Chapter 5, you learned to ask the right questions. You uncovered the real problem—the root cause behind the request. No more building the wrong things for the wrong audience and finding out after they've gone to production.

In Chapter 6, you built the story. You sat with stakeholders, aligned on the goal, identified the key metrics, surfaced the insights, and agreed on the action. Everyone left the room on the same page. No more "that's not what I asked for" when you go to launch.

In Chapter 7, you designed your first Goal Banner and Decision Tile. Yeah! You took the storyboard, converted it into a 4-tile dashboard—structured for how our brains actually work. You built for speed to decision. No more analysis paralysis.

Three steps. One framework.

Now you're just one step away from completing the framework: delivery.

Presenting with confidence may be the last step, but it's a skill that's woven throughout the entire system.

Here's what most people miss: at every step of the framework, you need to present—your questions, your findings, your designs—to stakeholders for feedback and approval.

Taking a step back.

In Chapter 5, you asked discovery questions. While you may have done it via email in some cases due to your company's culture, you may have had to set up a formal meeting to ask a group of stakeholders those questions. You likely put them on a slide deck and started presenting.

In Chapter 6, you facilitated the storyboard session. You had to guide the conversation, handle disagreement, and build consensus. Every time you read the storyboard, you were presenting.

In Chapter 7, you designed a dashboard. Maybe a slide deck. But you didn't build it in isolation. You had to present mockups, get feedback, and iterate based on their reactions.

Every single touch point required delivery skills.

These frequent, seemingly harmless interactions? They're huge points of failure if they are not handled correctly.

It's literally the difference between success and failure, and most professionals don't even see it happening. Scary.

They keep talking when someone is confused. They get defensive when someone pushes back on an insight. They rush through the action slide when that's the whole point.

DESIGN—VISUALS THAT DRIVE ACTION

The dashboard or slide deck was perfect. The delivery killed it.

In Chapter 8, you will learn how to handle these critical touch points—how to build trust, create buy-in, and, ultimately, drive action.

You'll learn how to spot the Three Signs of Influence to tell you in real time whether your stakeholders are with you or tuning out.

It's a delicate dance, but one that can be mastered with a system, intention, and practice.

The visual is ready. Now let's make sure you are, too.

You didn't just design a dashboard. You designed a decision. That's what Decision Drivers do.

It's time to present with confidence—that you're being seen, heard, and understood.

CHAPTER EIGHT

DELIVER— PRESENT TO WIN BUY-IN

"People will forget what you said, people will forget what you did, but people will never forget how you made them feel."
—Maya Angelou

The butterflies weren't the problem. The jet lag was.

I had just flown into Melbourne after having an amazing Thanksgiving with my family in Lisbon. Jet-lagged. Exhausted. But I figured it was fine—I'd pushed through fatigue before. I knew the material.

I was wrong.

Standing on stage, staring at the slides, my mind was blank.

Nothing came to mind.

The words on the screen were all I could get out of my mouth.

Word. For. Word.

Full robot mode. In front of 600 people.

I was horrified. I watched their faces change—from confusion to boredom to scrolling on their phones. I couldn't stop it. My brain was running on fumes, so I just kept reading the screen to burn the time.

Fight-or-flight mode kicked in. And flight won.

I barely mumbled something at the end about "that's the key takeaway," then hauled my butt out of there before anyone could ask questions.

I will never forget that keynote. It was the worst one in my life. I felt horrible. These people flew in from across the country. They gave me their time. And I gave them a robot presenter reading text off the slides.

Even as a veteran global keynote speaker, I froze.

It wasn't just exhaustion. I had worked through that before.

Something weird happened before I got on stage. I started to second-guess myself. Why?

I was determined to find out and never let it happen again.

According to the National Institute of Mental Health, approximately 77% of professionals experience fear before public speaking. Data professionals? Even worse. Roughly two-thirds of us experience some form of impostor syndrome. We don't even feel like we belong in the room.

That voice asking, "What if I'm not enough?" doesn't show up once. It rears its ugly head every single time we walk into a room to present.

Add exhaustion, stress, or fear to the mix, and our brain does something crazy: it goes into survival mode.

That's what happened to me in Melbourne.

When my brain checked out, I did what most people do without even realizing it: I started talking *at* them instead of *to* them.

That keynote still haunts me to this day. But it wasn't the last time I saw it happen.

I started noticing it from the other side—as the stakeholder. Sitting in meetings, watching smart people—who know their stuff—freezing up. Reading slides word for word. Losing the room without even realizing.

It was painful to watch. Even more painful to hear. Because I knew exactly what was happening.

I caught myself tuning out. Checking my phone. Quietly questioning their credibility. Watching minute by minute until it was time to leave.

If I was doing it, everyone else in the room was too.

I was now my audience in Melbourne. Ouch.

That's when it hit me—how fragile trust is. One bad touchpoint. A presentation. A dashboard review. A failed status update. That's all it takes. Your reputation. Your credibility. Your ability to get buy-in—down the drain.

It's a delicate dance, and one that has to be mastered.

Because when you don't, the damage goes far beyond one bad meeting.

DEATH BY A THOUSAND TOUCHPOINTS

Projects don't die in a bubble. They die slowly—one touchpoint at a time.

Every time you present your work, you're delivering. You're either building trust or losing it. There's no in-between.

And here's what most people miss: Delivery isn't just the final presentation. Delivery is every single touchpoint in the framework:

- The discovery discussion, where you confirm context
- The storyboard reviews, where you align stakeholders
- The design walkthroughs, where you show dashboard prototypes
- The status updates, the "check-ins," the "quick syncs"
- And yes, the final sign-off

Each one is a chance to gain or lose buy-in. Each one is a test. And most people don't even realize they're being graded.

Here's the hard truth: 88% of data projects die somewhere along this path. Not because of bad data. Not because of ugly dashboards. Because trust eroded one touchpoint at a time.

Maybe it was the dashboard walkthrough where you talked for 40 minutes and never asked a single question, thinking everyone was following along.

Maybe it was the storyboard review where stakeholders zoned out and you didn't notice.

You didn't lose them at the end. You lost them along the way.

And here's what makes it worse: corporate posturing.

Polite nods. Quiet thank-yous. "Looks great, thanks for sharing."

It screams "all is well" until you discover absolutely no one is using what you built.

You lost them somewhere. You just didn't see it.

It's a vicious cycle. The feedback loop is broken. Nobody tells you when you're losing the room. They just disengage quietly. Check their phones. Start answering emails. Nod politely until the meeting ends.

And you walk out thinking, "That went well."

Meanwhile, your credibility is taking hits you can't see. The "go-to" status you've been building is slipping away. Your reputation for getting things done "right" is eroding—one touchpoint at a time.

There are a dozen reasons touchpoints fail. Poor prep. Bad timing. Nerves. Wrong audience. Unclear objectives. Too much data. Not enough context.

But here is what they all have in common: The moment something feels off, we turn inward. We focus on ourselves. We stop watching our audience.

We miss the confused faces. The glazed eyes. The polite nods that mean nothing.

We start coasting in auto mode.

And that's when it happens. You stop talking *to* the room—and start talking *at* them.

It's a silent killer. But once you see yourself doing it, you can't unsee it.

The question is: Do you know what talking *to* them actually looks like?

TALK *TO* PEOPLE, NOT *AT* THEM

For a long time, I thought I was bad at presenting. Turns out, I wasn't bad at all. I was just doing what I had been trained to do.

August 28, 1963. Lincoln Memorial.

250,000 people. The most important speech of his career.

Martin Luther King Jr. had his remarks prepared on a few typewritten pages. Words he'd carefully crafted.

He started reading them to the huge crowd.

Powerful lines about injustice. About discrimination. About the urgent moment.

But something wasn't clicking.

He stood at the podium giving a lecture. Reading his notes. Delivering powerful words. And the crowd just listened. Polite. Attentive. But clearly not on board.

According to observers that day, the speech was failing to resonate like his other, more noteworthy sermons. Civil rights leader John Lewis said King himself could sense he was falling short.

That's when something extraordinary happened. Mahalia Jackson, the gospel singer standing behind him, shouted, "Tell 'em about the dream, Martin!"

It was like something snapped in King. Pushing his notes aside, he stopped reading.

"I have a dream, that one day...."

He shifted from lecturer to preacher. From talking at the crowd to talking to them—about his dreams, his vision of the future. And 250,000 people came alive.

That simple shift created one of the greatest speeches ever made.

Here's what most people miss about that moment: The words didn't change MLK's impact. The connection did.

When he stopped reading and started speaking and watching, the crowd came alive. They were becoming a part of his vision.

Similarly, when we are presenting to audiences—whether it's during a storyboarding session, a dashboard review, or a status update—we tend to stick to the script. Talking at people versus talking to them.

When you talk at people: You walk in, pull up slides, and read: "As you can see, the current state shows 1,247 tickets. . ."

When you talk to people: You walk in, make eye contact, and say: "We're here to decide whether we're fixing the support ticket crisis or not. Right now, we're drowning in 1,247 tickets a week. That's killing the team. If we cut that to 800 by March 15, we give them back half their time. That's what we're deciding today."

Then you pause. Watch their faces. See if they're nodding.

If they are, keep going.

If they're not, stop—"I'm seeing some confusion. Let me clarify. . ."

See the difference? One is a monologue. The other is a conversation.

Talking at people = information delivery. One-way. Scripted. Robot mode.

Talking to people = conversation. Two-way. Responsive. Human.

That's why so many data projects fail. Not because the project is bad, but because of failed communication. Stakeholders are being talked at instead of to—at every single touchpoint.

By the time they reach sign-off, it's a formality.

Polite nods instead of "here are our next steps."

No trust = no buy-in.

Now you see the difference. The question: how do you stay on the right side of it?

STEP 4: PRESENT TO WIN BUY-IN

Here's how to stay on the right side of it.

Not by calming your nerves. Not by practicing more. Not by memorizing your script.

By following a structure that keeps you focused on them—not yourself—even when everything in you wants to retreat to robot mode.

Talking at them = robot mode. Reading slides. Praying it ends.

Talking to them = human mode. Reading faces. Driving decisions.

But that's not the hard part.

Every presenter knows this. They know connection matters. They know reading slides kills engagement.

And yet.

Melbourne happened to me. It probably happened to you, too.

The issue isn't knowledge. It's habit. It's pressure. It's that moment when something feels off and your brain turns inward instead of staying locked on them.

So the real question isn't "How do I calm my nerves?" It's "How do I stay focused on them—consistently—whether I'm nervous, confident, exhausted, or under pressure?"

That's what this step is about.

In Chapter 7, you learned how to build your slides—a Goal Banner, three Decision Tiles, using the same structure as the dashboard. The design is done.

But don't confuse slides with delivery.

A great dashboard doesn't guarantee sign-off. A beautiful deck doesn't guarantee buy-in.

This step isn't just about the final deck or delivery meeting. It applies to every time you open your mouth to present to a stakeholder and move a decision forward.

This step gives you two things:

- **Structure:** How to deliver focused on your audience.
- **Measurement:** How to know, in real time, if they're with you.

No more guessing. No more hoping. No more walking out wondering if it landed.

It's about what you say, how you say it, and what you watch for while saying it.

By the end of this section, you'll have a repeatable formula you can use in every presentation, every touchpoint, every conversation where buy-in matters.

Here's the structure.

The Opening: Win Trust in 60 Seconds

Every presentation starts the same way.

Your audience decides whether or not they will trust you in the first 30–60 seconds. This initial buy-in of your character is critical to your success.

It happens fast. It's emotional. It's gut-level.

If they trust you, they lean in. If they don't, they tune out. They might listen, but they won't act.

Yet so many presenters waste those precious 60 seconds on themselves:

"Thanks for having me..."

"I know everyone's busy..."

"Let me share my screen..."

You're focused on you. Your nerves. Your screen. Your apologies.

Meanwhile, your audience makes a snap judgment: This person is not ready or sure. Not confident. I'm not following them.

That's it. That's how quickly trust is lost.

Here's how to win it instead.

Step 1: Start with a Short Greeting, Then State Their Need (10 seconds)

Start with a brief acknowledgment, then immediately state the decision and level of urgency.

"Good morning, everyone. We're here to decide if we're fixing the support ticket crisis or not."

Notice what you didn't do:

- You didn't apologize for taking their time.
- You didn't fumble with your screen.
- You didn't talk about yourself.

Instead, you focused on them—their problem, their decision.

Now pause. Scan the room.

Check for Sign #1: Clarity.

Are they nodding? Do they understand what decision has to be made? Nods? Move on. No nods? Confusion? Stop.

"I'm seeing some confusion. Let me clarify what we're here to decide..."

Don't move forward without clarity. If they don't understand what they're deciding, nothing else you say will matter.

Get clarity on the decision before moving forward.

Step 2: Show Why It Matters (20 seconds)

State the stakes. State the goal. Focus on what's in it for them.

"Right now, we're drowning in 1,247 tickets a week. It's killing the team. If we work to cut that down to 800 tickets a week by March 15 (3 months), we will drastically improve customer satisfaction and reduce turnover. We need to decide today if we will work together to do so."

Notice the language:

- "We're drowning"—not "the data shows."
- "It's killing the team"—emotional stakes, not just numbers.
- "We need to decide today"—urgency, not open-ended.

Now pause. Scan the room.

Check for Sign #1 and Sign #2.

Are they nodding at the goal? Do they understand what cutting down to 800 tickets a week by March means? Good—they have clarity.

Are they asking questions? "Why 800?" "How'd we land on that number?" "Is March realistic?"

Bingo. You have buy-in. They're engaging with the target. They're mentally trying it on. This is good—even if the questions sound challenging.

Nods and questions? Move on. No nods? Resistance? Stop and ask.

"I'm sensing the 800 target feels off. What concerns are coming up?"

Get clarity and buy-in on the goal before moving forward.

Step 3: Set Expectations (30 seconds)

Draw a clear path with no surprises, so the brain knows what's coming.

I'll walk you through where we are, what's blocking us, and the three actions we need to take. This will take 30–45 minutes, with 10 minutes for questions.

Why this matters: When the brain knows the structure, it can relax and listen. When it doesn't know what's coming, it stays on guard—waiting for surprises instead of processing your content.

Pause, scan the room, and check for all three Signs of Influence.

Nods? They have clarity on the expectations.

Questions? "Will we cover who owns each action?" That's buy-in on the process.

Timeline language? "What's the implementation timeline?" "When would we start?" That's Sign #3: Action readiness. They're already thinking about doing it.

All three signs present? Then proceed.

Any sign missing? Stop. Trace back.

No clarity = no buy-in. No buy-in = no action.

Fix it before you move forward. Never proceed through a gate without the sign.

The key: confirm all three signs in the first 60 seconds.

Once you have all three Signs of Influence, they're ready to listen.

Now you need to keep them.

The Delivery Formula: Stay in Human Mode

This is where most presenters lose the room. And they have no idea it's even happening.

They nail the opening, then slip into autopilot. Robot mode kicks in. Twenty minutes later, they look up and everyone's checked out.

Sound familiar?

That's exactly what happened to me in Melbourne. I started strong. Then I turned inward. Stopped watching. Started reading the slides. Robot mode.

The key is to stay in human mode. This formula will help you do that. It keeps your brain locked on your audience—even when you're tired, nervous, or under pressure.

Five simple steps. Repeat each step for every section of your presentation.

Step 1: Say the Content

Don't read the screen. Tell them the story while watching their faces.

The moment you start reading slides, you stop reading the room. And the moment you stop reading the room, you're flying blind.

Your slides are for *them* to reference, not for *you* to read. If you need notes, use speaker notes or a printed outline. But your eyes should be on faces, not screens.

Step 2: Pause

Two to three seconds. This feels like forever. Do it anyway.

Let their brains process. Look around the room.

This is where most presenters fail—they rush from point to point because silence feels uncomfortable. But silence is where processing happens. Silence is where you *read*.

Here's what I tell my students: if it doesn't feel awkward, you didn't pause long enough. A real pause—one where you actually look around the room and scan faces—should feel slightly uncomfortable. That discomfort is your signal that you're doing it right.

The pause is also your reset button. Every time you pause, you break the autopilot loop. You pull yourself out of robot mode and back into human mode. Without pauses, you're just a machine running through slides. With pauses, you're a human having a conversation.

Step 3: Ask Yourself a Question About Them

Not "Am I explaining this well?"

But "Do *they* still have it?"

This tiny shift keeps your brain focused outward instead of spiraling inward. It's the antidote to robot mode.

Other questions to ask yourself:

- "Are they still nodding?"
- "Who looks confused?"
- "Has anyone checked their phone?"
- "Is the energy still there?"

You're not asking them these questions. You're asking yourself—while you pause and scan.

Step 4: Watch for the Three Signs of Influence

- **Sign #1—Clarity:** Are they nodding?
- **Sign #2—Buy-In:** Are they asking questions? Are they leaning in?
- **Sign #3—Action:** Are they mentioning timelines? Taking notes?

This is your real-time feedback system. No more guessing if it's working. No more waiting until the end to find out you lost them on slide three.

Step 5: Adjust Based on What You See

Not nodding? Back up. Clarify.

"I want to make sure that landed. Let me put it another way. . ."

No questions? Invite them.

"What concerns are coming up?"

"What am I missing from your perspective?"

Energy dropping? Make it concrete.

"What would this look like for your team specifically?"

"Let's pause on this—how does this connect to what you're dealing with right now?"

Doubt surfacing? Address it now.

"I'm sensing some hesitation. What's on your mind?"

"I see some skepticism. Let's talk about it."

Don't wait until the end. By then, it's too late. The corporate politeness has already kicked in. They'll nod, say "looks great," and ignore everything you said.

Figure 8.1 The delivery formula

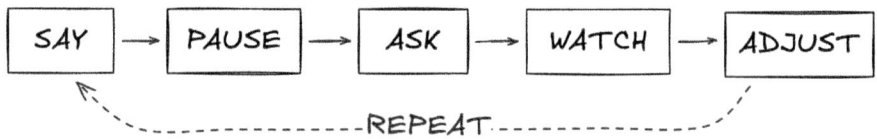

Here's the formula (Figure 8.1): Say → Pause → Ask → Watch → Adjust

That's the cure to robot mode.

This is how you stay in human mode—even under pressure. Even when exhausted. Even when the stakes are high.

It keeps you focused on them. This is how you build trust. This is how you win buy-in.

The formula doesn't just structure your delivery; it structures your attention.

The Closing: Provide Clear Next Steps

You've maintained all three signs through your presentation. Your audience has clarity. They're bought in.

Now lock in what happens next.

Not every touchpoint needs a major decision. Discovery sessions need confirmation. Storyboard reviews need alignment. Design walkthroughs need feedback. Status updates need agreement on next steps.

But whatever the touchpoint, you need to leave with something concrete: an action, a decision, a clear next step with an owner and a deadline.

This is the moment of truth. Everything you've built—the opening, the formula, the sign-watching—it all comes down to this. Do they act, or do they nod politely and forget about it by tomorrow?

Most people blow it at the end.

"Any questions?"

"I'll send you the deck."

Vague. Weak. Not clear on what comes next.

The close is where buy-in becomes action.

Here's how to close:

"Before we wrap, let's confirm the next steps. Anna, you're updating the help center articles by Friday at 5:00 p.m. Hunter, you're fixing the password reset by Monday at 9:00 a.m. Charlotte, you're creating the FAQ by Wednesday at noon. Does that work for everyone?"

Notice what you did:

- You named people directly (creates accountability).
- You gave specific deadlines with times (avoids ambiguity).
- You asked for confirmation (forces response).

Here's how it works for other touchpoints in the framework:

- **Discovery close:** "So we're aligned—the real problem is self-service, not ticket volume. By Friday, you'll send me last quarter's data, and we'll schedule the storyboard session for Monday. Does that work?"

- **Storyboard close:** "We're aligned on the three-part story: problem, metrics, actions. By Monday, you'll review the draft with your team. We finalize Tuesday. Any concerns before then?"
- **Design close:** "The dashboard structure works. By Wednesday, we test with three users from your team. You'll send me their names by end of day. Good?"
- **Status update close:** "We're on track for March 15. The one blocker is the API integration—Hunter, you're escalating that by tomorrow at noon. Anything else before we break?"

Same structure. Different content. Always a clear next step.

Watch for Sign #3 one last time:

"When would we launch?"

"Let me check my calendar."

"Could we push the deadline to Thursday?"

Boom. Sign #3 confirmed. Timeline language means commitment is forming. They're not thinking about *if* anymore; they're thinking about *when*.

Not hearing timeline language? Ask directly.

"What would it take to commit to these next steps?"

Listen for what comes back.

Logistics? Help them solve it.

"What resources do you need to make this happen?"

Doubt? That's a Sign #2 problem. Trace back.

"What concerns haven't we addressed?"

Silence? That's a Sign #1 problem. Trace back further.

"Let me make sure we're aligned on what we're deciding here."

No clarity = no buy-in. No buy-in = no action.

Trace back, find the broken sign, and fix it.

No maybes. Leave with a clear next step.

A QUICK REFERENCE TO THE FORMULA

Opening (60 seconds)
- Step 1: State the decision → Check for Clarity.
- Step 2: State the stakes and goal → Check for Clarity + Buy-In.
- Step 3: Set expectations → Check for all three signs.

Middle (main content)
- Say → Pause → Ask → Watch → Adjust.
- Repeat for every section.
- Maintain all three signs throughout.

Close (next step)
- Specific actions + owners + deadlines.
- Lock in Sign #3 with timeline language.
- No maybes. Leave with commitment.

This works for every presentation in the framework: Discover. Define. Design. Deliver.

You now don't just know what to say; you know how to measure if it's working—in real time.

WHY IT WORKS

Day one of my workshops is do-or-die for me and my team.

Three days. Mostly Fortune 500 companies. Shell. Nestlé. Amazon. Abbott.

Most attendees walked in thinking data storytelling means designing prettier dashboards and reports. A few came ready to learn. The rest? Tagged along because their boss made them. Sigh.

Five minutes in, I could do what most trainers do. Pull up my slide deck. Introduce myself. Explain the agenda. Talk at them about what I'm going to teach.

And I used to do this.

Now I don't.

Instead, I scan the room, find the most skeptical faces, and ask: "Raise your hand if you've ever built a dashboard that nobody used."

Every hand goes up. Even Mr. Skeptical in the back.

"Keep your hand up if you have no idea why that happened."

Most hands stay up. A few people laugh.

"That's why we're here. By the end of this workshop, you'll know exactly why your dashboards get abandoned—and how to fix it."

I pause and watch the room shift.

I look for Sign #1: Clarity. Do they understand why we're here and the problem we're going to solve?

Heads are nodding. Good. They get it.

Then I go one step further: "Here's what nobody told you. The problem isn't your data. It's not your design. It's that you were never taught how to get true buy-in."

I look straight at Mr. Skeptical. Arms crossed. But he's listening now.

If I don't get his and everyone else's buy-in in the first few minutes, it's game over. They're gone. Not physically, but mentally.

They start checking emails. "Urgent call" in the afternoon.

"You—what's your biggest frustration with stakeholders?"

Mr. Skeptical doesn't expect to be called on. He sits up and uncrosses his arms.

"They ask for something. I build it. They change their minds, I rebuild, and so the story goes."

"Exactly. I bet you were never sure if you had their full buy-in before you built. That's what we're fixing this week."

He leans forward, picks up his pen.

He's bought in.

Here's what just happened.

I didn't convince him with a lecture. I didn't wow him with credentials. I asked a question about him, listened to his answer, and connected my solution to his problem.

I talked *to* him, not *at* him.

That shift—from broadcast to conversation—changes everything.

And it's not just my experience talking. Research backs this up.

In 1988, Michael T. Motley's research on communication styles found that a "conversation voice" directly correlates with trust, satisfaction, and commitment. Not "might help." It correlates measurably.

When people feel like you're talking with them, they trust you more. They engage more. They commit more.

When they feel talked at? They tune out. Start scrolling on their phones. Hear nothing you say.

Every time you resort to reading slides instead of faces, you're killing trust.

Every time you dive into monologue mode without pausing, you're killing engagement.

Every time you present talking at instead of talking to them, you're killing buy-in.

Simple as that. The formula keeps you focused on the room and not yourself. Each step forces your attention on your audience.

Mr. Skeptical from day one?

By that afternoon, he was the first one to volunteer for our class role-play exercise. He presented his dashboard to the room, tested the formula, and got great feedback.

He even noted to me after, "I had no idea I was talking at people or that you could measure buy-in. Wow. It changes the game for presentations."

This is common feedback.

Once you see it, you can't unsee it.

Now go make them see you.

WHEN YOU LOSE THE ROOM

Your brain will lie to you. Mine did in Melbourne.

The second you feel the energy drop—phones appearing, eyes glazing, that weird silence—your brain will whisper: Keep going. Don't acknowledge it. Maybe they're just tired. It's not you.

It is you.

And the next lie gets even worse. Speed up. Get through the rest. The next slide will get a better response.

It won't.

Here's what to do instead: first diagnose, then fix.

But before you diagnose anything, do a self-check.

Are you talking to them or at them?

Are you reading the slides or providing context? Rattling through data? Presenting instead of conversing? If so, the fix starts with you.

Now find the broken sign.

- **Sign 1—Clarity:** Looks like furrowed brows. Blank stares. "Can you say that again?" They don't get it. You've been talking at them. Shift. Stop and say, "Let me put that another way." Simplify. Fewer words. One concrete example.
- **Sign 2—Buy-In:** Looks like arms crossed. Leaning back. Polite nods but zero questions. They get it. They don't want it. Stop and say, "I'm sensing hesitation. What concerns are coming up?" Shut up. Listen. Their objection is your roadmap back.

- **Sign 3—Action:** Looks like phones out. Side conversations. "I have to jump to another call." They're gone. Stop and say, "I'm losing you. What do you actually need from this meeting?"

These are all red flags that you can fix as you go.

Remember the rule: the signs build. No clarity = no buy-in. No buy-in = no action.

Always fix the broken sign before moving forward.

TRY THIS MONDAY

It's time to use the formula.

Before your next presentation—any presentation, really—do this:

Write your 60-second opening. On paper or in your phone notes.

Three parts:

- **The decision (10 seconds):** What are we here to decide? One sentence. No jargon.
- **The stakes (20 seconds):** Why should they care? What happens if we don't act?
- **The expectations (30 seconds):** What will you cover? How long will it take?

That's your opening.

Now say it out loud.

Find someone—a colleague, a friend—anyone will do. Deliver your opening while watching their face.

Did they follow without asking you to clarify? That's clarity.

Did it sound like a conversation—or a script?

Did you get through it without reading anything?

Now ask them two questions:

"What decision did I just set up?"

"Why should you care?"

If they can answer both without guessing, you're ready. If not, back to the drawing board.

You'll know it's working when:

- You can state the decision without reading anything.
- You can explain the stakes without rattling off numbers.
- You can set expectations without saying, "I'll walk you through the deck."

When your opening feels like a conversation instead of a script, you've got it.

Practice until it's automatic. Then walk into your next meeting and watch what happens.

Getting buy-in early is key.

You'll feel the difference. So will they.

YOU MADE IT!

You have the complete framework:

1. **Discover:** Ask questions to reveal the true context.
2. **Define:** Build storyboards that align stakeholders.
3. **Design:** Create visuals that drive action.
4. **Deliver:** Present to win.

Four steps. One system. The ability to measure buy-in at every stage. The ability to turn your insights into action.

But here's what you need to remember: this isn't a presentation technique; it's a professional survival skill.

In the age of AI, the analysis will get automated. The dashboards will build themselves. The insights will surface faster than humans can even imagine.

What won't get automated is you—the human in the room.

AI can surface insights, but it can't build trust; it can't sit across from a skeptical CFO, read the hesitation, address the real concern, and get the yes.

That's you—the Decision Driver. That's your job now.

You just learned how to do it.

Follow the four steps. Watch for the Three Signs of Influence. Adjust when you lose them.

You'll mess up the first few times—that's fine. Progress over perfection.

What you'll notice immediately is the difference in how your audience responds: less back-and-forth, fewer "let's circle back" meetings, more trust, more action.

While everyone else stays hoping their insights drive action, you'll know because you can measure it in real time.

In Chapter 9, I'll introduce some folks who put this framework to the test. Real business and data professionals, just like you. Real stakes. They took the leap and won. Let me show you how they did it.

CHAPTER NINE

MASTERY—THE 90-DAY PATH

"Knowing is not enough; we must apply. Willing is not enough; we must do."

—Goethe

Order-takers hope their work lands. Decision Drivers know before they leave the room.

Mastery isn't about more hours. It's about seeing the patterns others miss—and acting on them.

I've shown you the method. Now let me prove it works for everyone.

Meet John.

JOHN: THE WRONG PROBLEM

"Thanks, John. Send the deck."

John's mouth went dry.

He looked up from his laptop. The CFO was scrolling on his phone. Two VPs were whispering to each other. Someone in the back had closed their laptop and was staring at the ceiling.

Six weeks of work. Fifteen iterations. And that's it?

His stomach dropped. He mumbled something about following up and started gathering his things. The room was already clearing out before he finished packing his bag.

No discussion. No debate. No decision. Just... send the deck.

Translation: We're done here. And nothing's going to happen.

Four words. That's all he got after six grueling weeks of work.

John was a quiet financial analyst at a midsized manufacturing company, three years into his career—brilliant with numbers, not so much with speaking.

If you look at his spreadsheets, he's a rockstar. If you watch him present, you'd never know.

He struggled to articulate his own findings, hated speaking in front of others, and suffered from constant impostor syndrome. *What if I'm not technical enough? What if they don't believe my analysis?*

Sound familiar?

One day, John got a big assignment—straight from the CFO himself: a deep cost-reduction analysis for next year's planning cycle. He would present his findings to the entire financial leadership team.

John did what he always did. He buried himself in analysis mode—iterating, refining, revising, updating. Fifteen versions of the same spreadsheet. Classic analysis paralysis.

Now he was standing in the hallway outside that conference room, holding a laptop bag full of "perfect" analysis that nobody would use.

John knew something had gone wrong. He just wasn't sure what.

He sent a follow-up email the next day. Crickets.

That's when he decided to do something different.

John showed up to the workshop with a look I've seen a thousand times; defeat, frustration, a little desperation.

He was mostly quiet for the first half of the day—listening, taking some notes.

But when I started teaching the Discovery section, I watched his posture change—he uncrossed his arms and leaned in.

A light bulb went off.

After class, he came up and said, "So basically... I've been building the wrong thing this whole time?"

I looked at him and smiled. "That's a great question. It means you're ready to stop guessing and start asking the right questions."

That night, he almost didn't book the call with his CFO. He told me later: "What if he thinks I'm wasting his time? What if he wonders why I didn't ask this 10 weeks ago?"

He sent it anyway.

The next morning—before Day Two even started—John was on a video call with his CFO.

He asked the three discovery questions:

"What does success look like in six months?"

"If we could only fix three cost drivers, which ones matter most?"

"If this project worked perfectly, what would you tell the board?"

The CFO leaned back.

"Honestly? I only care about three cost drivers: labor, freight, and scrap. Everything else is noise."

After 10 weeks of analysis, he finally discovered what actually mattered.

John walked into Day Two like a different person—he had struck gold.

I overheard him telling another attendee, "My call took 15 minutes, and now I finally understand what he actually cares about. Crazy how that works."

As we moved into the Define step, he turned that conversation into a storyboard—no charts, no visuals, just the story: the goal, the key metrics, where each metric was leaking money, and three specific actions with owners and dates.

On Day Three, he volunteered to present his storyboard to the class for feedback. It was clear, easy to understand, and ready for action.

When he returned to the office that Monday, he walked into the CFO's office and shared the storyboard.

The CFO leaned forward. "Perfect. Now how do we build this out to help the team drive down costs?"

Two days later, John rebuilt his entire report. It took him less time to build the new version than it took to color-code the old one.

His next presentation was to the same room—same audience, same people who gave him "send the deck" three weeks earlier.

This time, John walked in with confidence.

One: he already had the CFO on board—pre-aligned.

Two: he knew what signs to watch for to ensure that he was getting buy-in.

The CFO was highly engaged, even adding his own input after each slide. The team started asking, "How can we…?" and "Will this help us…?"

John's next steps were questioned, then accepted. The team put together a timeline for how and when to execute the next steps. The CFO signed off on the spot.

The same report went to the board the following month—presented, blessed, funded.

To no one's surprise, 6 months later, John got promoted.

When asked about it, he said, "I've always been better with spreadsheets than people. But this gave me a way to connect without pretending to be someone I'm not. I just follow the process, and it works."

Loved that: "I just follow the process, and it works."

Introvert. Spreadsheet geek. Same John—different outcome.

The framework doesn't change who you are. It gives you a system that works regardless of who you are.

If you work the method, it will work for you.

The smarter you are, the easier it is to hide behind your work. Analysis feels safe. No one gets fired for being thorough.

But influence isn't about being thorough. It's about being relevant.

Most analysts don't fail because their work is wrong. They fail because they solved a problem no one had.

That's why stakeholders say, "Thanks. Just send the deck," and move on—not because they disagree, but because they never saw themselves in the story.

The framework shows you how to catch this early—before putting in weeks of effort like John.

But what if you're not an introvert hiding behind spreadsheets? What if you're a leader—confident, articulate, commanding—and you're still not getting buy-in?

Meet Nadina.

NADINA: THE EVERYONE PROBLEM

If John was quiet and analytical, Nadina was quite the opposite—bold, confident, articulate, and she commanded every room she walked into.

As Director of Analytics at a major oil and gas company, she led a team of brilliant people. Their dashboards were stunning—technically sophisticated, visually clean.

They even told stories. Or so she thought.

So why was nobody using them?

Operations complained that the data was too high level. Finance said it was too detailed. Safety said it was missing context entirely.

Same dashboard. Three different expectations.

This was after weeks of gathering requirements, months of design reviews, and endless alignment meetings.

Now the dashboards were live.

Nobody was using them.

Nadina was frustrated.

Every time she thought they were done, another executive popped up: "Can we add one more view? I feel like we need to see this too."

Add this metric. Add that filter. Add another slice.

Her team was fried. They'd given up pushing back—strictly in order-taking mode, just building whatever they were asked.

She had to make it stop.

And Nadina? She was stuck in the middle—absorbing complaints from above, shielding her team below, running on caffeine and frustration.

By the time she showed up to our workshop with most of her data team, you could see it on their faces: burned out, overwhelmed, and defeated.

They sat in the front row, listening intently.

When I started teaching the Storyboarding section, Nadina raised her hand.

"We already have dashboards. They already tell a story. We're way past this step."

I smiled. "Do they tell a story, or do they just have well-designed charts arranged in an order?"

She paused.

I said, "Here's a test: Can you write down—in one sentence—what decision each dashboard is supposed to drive? Not what data it shows. What decision."

She nodded.

During lunch, I saw her in the corner with her team—whiteboards out, sticky notes everywhere.

They were trying to answer the question.

When Nadina walked into the room the next day, something had changed.

She was lighter—smiling, even a bit confused.

Before I even started teaching, she said, "We couldn't do it. We couldn't write the sentence."

Translation. We thought we had a story. We had none.

Here's what the storyboard exercise revealed:

Operations cared about uptime.

Safety cared about incident-free days.

Finance cared about cost per barrel.

The dashboards weren't broken—the audience was. Three completely different definitions of success.

She's been trying to cram all of them into one dashboard. No wonder it failed.

There was no story—just well-designed charts on a screen with good information.

They were arguing about colors and filters. Nobody ever asked, "What the one decision this should drive?"

A storyboard would have caught this on Day One.

Nadina didn't waste time.

Before leaving the workshop, she had her team start building three separate storyboards—one per group. She booked meetings with each—separately—for the following week.

Operations first. Then Safety. Then Finance.

Each storyboard had one storyline, one definition of success, one decision to drive—built from their own words.

Operations: "How can we drive more uptime?"

Safety: "How can we boost incident-free days?"

Finance: "How can we reduce cost per barrel?"

No visuals yet. Just stories.

When she got back to the office, she ran three storyboard sprints instead of one giant alignment circus.

She showed each group their storyboard—no dashboards, no charts, just the story.

She asked, "Is this the decision you need to make? Are these the right metrics to make it?"

In her words, "Buy-in was fast. Like, shockingly fast."

Operations: "Finally, we can see what slows us down without the noise."

Safety: "This is how we actually measure our good days."

Finance: "Now we can easily see where the dollars are leaking."

Over the next two weeks, her team raced to build three dashboards—one per audience, each anchored in a validated storyboard.

No rework. No politics. No more "Can we just add one more thing?"

Why? Because they'd already bought into the story. The dashboard just brought it to life.

The Operations dashboard became a daily pulse tool. The Safety dashboard went up on the big screens at the plant. The Finance dashboard made it into the board pack.

In our last conversation Nadina said something I will never forget: "The dashboard wasn't the deliverable. The story was."

She was right.

Without the story, dashboards are useless.

Bold leader. Complex organization. Political minefield. Same framework. Same result.

John learned to ask the right questions.

Nadina learned that dashboards don't create alignment. Stories do.

But what if you already have the story right? What if your data is solid, your slides are clear, and your delivery is sharp—and you still can't tell if any of it is landing?

Meet Cabria.

CABRIA: READING THE ROOM

Cabria wasn't shy. Wasn't unsure. Wasn't hiding behind spreadsheets. Quite the opposite.

She was a Sales Director at a fast-growing SaaS company—confident, sharp, the kind of person who drove action in her team by sheer force of will.

Her QBRs (quarterly business reviews) were tight, yet something was off.

She could never tell if her message was landing.

No questions. No debate. No pushback.

Just polite nods, "good deck," and… silence.

Cabria knew exactly what was at stake. QBRs aren't status updates. They're the one meeting each quarter where your job isn't to share what happened—it's to shape what happens next.

Her goal? Get leadership to approve her customer-retention strategy, fund her renewal programs, and green-light the resources she needed to hit next quarter's targets.

The numbers were solid—renewal rates, churn risk by segment, pipeline coverage, net revenue retention (NRR).

But the story was not sticking.

Leadership saw performance, not potential. Trends, not decisions.

And in this economy—where every dollar spent is tracked, questioned, and tied to ROI—"good deck" wasn't going to cut it.

She needed a commitment to her strategy, not compliments.

When Cabria joined our community, she was clear on what she wanted.

"I don't need help designing better slides. I don't need help with delivery. I already know how to own a room."

Fair enough.

"So, what do you need?"

I need to know if it's actually working. I present, they nod, and then nothing happens. I can't tell if I'm actually getting buy-in sometimes until it's too late.

When we got to the Three Signs of Influence, I watched her face change.

She stared at the big screen, then blurted out, "Wait—you can actually measure buy-in?"

She shook her head, half-laughing. "I've been tracking revenue, retention, and pipeline for years. It never occurred to me that buy-in was something you could measure too."

That's when it clicked.

She's been flying blind, hoping to gain buy-in.

The Three Signs of Influence give her a new lens.

Her next quarter's QBR was six weeks out, so she changed her approach.

First, she rebuilt the story—using the storyboard to strip out the noise and reorder her slides around the decisions she needed approved, not the data she wanted to show.

Then she focused on reading the room.

The QBR opened with the customer voice—renewal challenges, success stories, the emotional "why" behind the data. She then showed the data to prove it: churn risk by segment, pipeline coverage for renewals, and NRR projections tied to action plans.

Halfway through, she spotted it.

The CRO leaned back, arms crossed.

Old Cabria would've kept pushing—finished the deck, asked if they had any questions, and moved on.

The new Cabria paused.

"I'm sensing some hesitation. What part do you have questions on?"

The CRO uncrossed his arms.

"It's not hesitation. I just need to understand—is this retention play going to protect our margin? Or just slow down the churn?"

There it is.

She pivoted on the spot, reframing the slide around margin protection instead of customer churn.

The CRO nodded—the real nod.

She was back on track.

She was tracking all Three Signs of Influence—nodding, asking "we/us" questions, and discussing timelines.

It was like talking to a different audience.

And then—the moment she was waiting for.

The CRO asked, "When can we roll this out?"

Within 60 minutes, she had verbal approval on her entire plan—the same plan that had been "under review" for the last two quarters.

When I asked her what she did differently, she replied, "I didn't change my slides. I changed how I listened. Those three signs gave me real-time feedback. I could see when I was losing them—and I knew how to win them back."

Cabria learned to read the room, and she won.

John learned to ask the right questions. Nadina learned to build the story before the dashboard. Cabria learned to adjust in real time.

Three people. Three completely different personalities.

THE 90-DAY TRUTH

Right now, you're probably thinking, "That's great for them. But what about me?"

Everything John, Nadina, and Cabria learned—you just learned too.

So let me be straight with you.

Malcolm Gladwell says you need 10,000 hours to master anything.

He's right about concert violinists, NBA players, and brain surgeons.

But he's dead wrong about stakeholder influence.

You don't need 10,000 hours to learn to drive buy-in. You need about 90 days—with the right system and a bias toward action.

John proved it works for introverts. Nadina proved it works for leaders. Cabria proved it works for presenters.

Now it's your turn.

YOUR 90-DAY SYSTEM

Don't try to master everything at once.

Mastery isn't magic; it's method.

Master one step at a time—in the right order, with deliberate practice.

Here's the path. And before you overthink it—don't.

Weeks 1–4: Discovery

Week 1: Study.

Reread Chapter 5. Write down the three discovery questions. Practice saying them out loud. Sounds dumb. Works.

Trust me, the awkwardness is the point.

Week 2: Safe practice.

Use them in low-stakes meetings: team standups, one-on-ones with peers. Ask three discovery questions per meeting. Don't worry about perfect phrasing—just get comfortable asking.

(It will feel awkward. That's normal. Awkward means you're growing.)

Week 3: Real practice.

In actual stakeholder meetings, start with one question: "What does success look like in 90 days?" Watch how it changes the conversation.

This is the meeting that changes everything. Don't chicken out.

Week 4: Full session.

Run a complete discovery meeting: 30 minutes, one stakeholder, five to seven questions. Confirm what you heard at the end.

Success metric: The stakeholder says, "No one's ever asked me that before."

(When you hear those words—and you will—you'll know you've arrived.)

Weeks 5–8: Storyboarding

Week 5: Solo.

Take your discovery notes. Build a storyboard on your own—one page, four boxes: goal, metrics, insights, actions. That's it. Don't overcomplicate it.

Week 6: Review.

Share it with your stakeholder—30 minutes. Say, "I want to make sure I understood you correctly." Ask, "What am I missing?"

(This is where it clicks. They'll correct things you didn't even know were wrong. That's the point.)

Week 7: Collaborate.

Build the storyboard with them, not for them. Bring blank sticky notes. Let them move things around. Let them own it.

Yes, giving up control feels terrifying. That's how you know it's working.

Week 8: Multi-stakeholder.

Two stakeholders. Same room. Facilitate the conversation. Let them co-create the story.

Success metric: They leave saying, "I've never felt this aligned before."

(And you'll leave thinking: why didn't I do this from the start?)

Weeks 9–12: Three Signs of Influence

Week 9: Awareness.

During any presentation, watch for the Three Signs. Don't try to adjust yet—just notice. Are they nodding? Asking questions? Using timeline language? Keep a journal after each session.

You'll be shocked how much you've been missing.

Week 10: Spotting.

When you see a sign go negative, pause: "I'm sensing some confusion. Let me back up." You don't need perfect recovery—just practice stopping.

The hardest thing you'll ever do mid-presentation. Also the most powerful.

Week 11: Responding.

Practice the three resistance responses. Confusion—"Let me show you this another way." Skepticism—"What part doesn't match what you're seeing?" Deflection—"I hear you. Can we address this first?"

You won't nail it every time. That's not the point. The point is you're no longer guessing.

Week 12: Closing.

End every presentation with an explicit ask: "Do we have agreement to move forward?" "Who owns this by when?" Follow up within two hours with a written summary.

Success metric: 80% of your presentations end with a clear commitment. (Not 100%. 80%. Mastery isn't perfection. It's consistency.)

FOUR PITFALLS

Let me save you some pain. I've watched smart people self-sabotage in exactly four ways.

- **Pitfall 1:** "I'll start when I have more time."

    When's that? Next quarter? After your next terrible presentation? After AI takes half the jobs in your department? There's no perfect time. Use one discovery question in your next meeting—five seconds. That's your starting line.
- **Pitfall 2:** "Stakeholders are too busy for storyboards."

    They're not too busy. They're too busy for rework—too busy for alignment meetings that go nowhere, too busy for dashboards nobody uses. Thirty minutes of storyboarding saves a hundred hours of building the wrong thing. Do the math.
- **Pitfall 3:** "I'm not good at reading people."

    Good news: you don't need to be. The Three Signs of Influence aren't personality—they're pattern recognition, observable behaviors: nodding, question types, timeline language. You don't need emotional intelligence. You need eyes and ears. Anyone can learn to spot them.
- **Pitfall 4:** "I tried it once, and it didn't work."

    Once. You tried a completely new approach to influence—once—and declared it broken. You didn't learn Excel in one afternoon. You didn't master SQL in a single query. Every presentation is practice. Measure improvement, not perfection. Compare Week 1 to Week 12—night and day.

THE TRANSFORMATION

Remember where you started.

Chapter 1. The $777 billion problem. Insights ignored. Decisions unmade. Careers stuck.

You've come a long way.

You now have a system.

Discovery gives you clarity before you build.

Storyboarding gives you alignment before you design.

The Three Signs of Influence give you feedback before it's too late.

But here's what really changed: you!

Order-taker → Strategic partner.

Before: "Tell me what dashboard you want."

Now: "Let's figure out what decision you're trying to make."

Chart builder → Decision Driver.

Before: "Here are 47 metrics. Pick what you need."

Now: "Here are the 3 metrics that matter for your goal."

Push and hope → Measure and adjust.

Before: "I hope this lands."

Now: "I can see it's not landing. Let me adjust."

Technical expert → Influence expert.

Before: "My value is accurate analysis."

Now: "My value is driving action."

You're not someone who hopes data drives decisions. You're someone who makes it happen.

Mastery isn't knowing the method. It's trusting it when the room goes quiet.

That's the shift.

And once you see it, you can't unsee it.

The signs show up everywhere—meetings, emails, conversations with your kids.

You'll catch yourself reading rooms you didn't even know you were in. That's mastery.

FROM MASTERY TO MOVEMENT

Now that you've learned the method, you've got a 90-day system to make it yours.

But here's where the true transformation happens.

One person with these skills is powerful. An entire team? Unstoppable.

What if everyone on your team knew how to ask discovery questions?

What if every project started with a storyboard?

What if your whole organization could read the room and adjust in real time?

That's not a skill upgrade. That's a culture shift.

Right now, you have something your peers don't. You can see what they're guessing at. You can measure what they're hoping for. You can drive action while they're still hoping their slides land.

But one person—no matter how skilled—can only change so many rooms.

What happens when this becomes the standard? When "send the deck" becomes a "relic" When every meeting starts with a story, not a spreadsheet? When buy-in isn't something you hope for—it's something you build?

That's not a chapter. That's a manifesto.

And it starts now!

CHAPTER 10

THE MOVEMENT

I grew up in the Caribbean, where I never had to earn permission to belong. My mom was a lovely Aruban lady who was always optimistic and smiling. My dad was a Trinidadian mix of Asian and French who was always working. Between them, we grew up with about five languages.

Our house felt like the United Nations—food, accents, customs, and stories.

Diversity wasn't something you explained. It just... existed.

Then I entered Corporate America.

One of my first customer meetings in the United States was in New York. I remember it like yesterday.

Small room. Dull fluorescent lights. Dark walls. Five people sitting around an old wooden conference table, most triple my age.

As I opened my mouth, I could see and feel the room change.

A raised eyebrow.

A half-smile.

A glance up from a laptop.

My accent was a distraction.

My gender was a distraction.

My race was a distraction.

Before I even finished my first sentence, decisions were already made about whether I actually belonged in the room.

I didn't have the luxury of hoping the data would speak for itself. Hope is a privilege. I couldn't afford to "just be confident" and trust that my polished presentation would win the day.

So I had to figure it out quickly—how to keep the room focused on my data, not my differences. It came down to having influence—not because I wanted to, but because I had to.

I needed to learn how to get buy-in—how to make stakeholders act, not just smile and then do absolutely nothing with the data.

It took a former Navy SEAL named Derek to say what nobody else would: that I was great technically but couldn't read a room to save my life.

And nothing was ever the same.

I was walking into meetings, presenting my data, hoping something—anything—would stick. Typical push-and-hope mindset.

So I stopped hoping.

And I started watching, listening, and measuring.

Within months, things changed.

I wasn't the data analyst pushing dashboards anymore. I was a strategic partner—the one who could read the room, get buy-in, and drive decisions.

I'm not telling you this to impress you. I'm telling you this because I don't want anyone else to go through what I did.

Knowing how to drive buy-in isn't a "nice to have." It's the skill every business and data professional needs to master to survive in corporate.

And you? You've already started.

Think back to where you were when you picked up this book.

Maybe you were me in that New York boardroom—watching the VP lean back and say, "I'm not seeing what you're saying here."

Maybe you were John, standing in the hallway lugging a laptop loaded with reports no one asked for.

Maybe you were stuck building dashboards no one used, wondering why.

That was Chapter 1.

Now you're here.

Nine chapters ago, you didn't have a system. Now you do.

You've learned how to ask the right questions to unlock the real problem. How to storyboard alignment before you start to build. How to design visuals that drive decisions instead of confusion. How to present like a human—talking *to* people, not *at* them.

And the most important part? You can now measure influence while it's happening. The Three Signs: Clarity, Buy-in, and Action.

John went from "send the deck" to driving a $2.1 million decision in a few days. Joshua proved it could happen in 90 seconds.

That's the shift.

You stop being the person who reports what happened. You become the person whose insights drive action.

Your title doesn't change.

Your influence does.

WHAT ACTUALLY CHANGES

This isn't about owning decisions. It's about owning the space to ensure your work has impact.

You're still the data person. You still bring rigor, accuracy, and restraint. You still do the analysis. You still build the dashboards.

But here's what changes.

Your work doesn't stop at the insights anymore.

Instead of reporting what happened and hoping someone does something with it, you create decision readiness.

You surface the decisions people have been avoiding.

You lay out the cost of waiting.

You make the decision obvious—not by being pushy, but by being clear.

You learn to ask dual-channel questions that activate both logic and imagination—cutting through the noise.

You learn to design visuals that drive decisions, not just display data.

You learn to talk TO your stakeholders, not AT them.

You learn to tell when someone's nodding because they understand and when they're nodding because they want you to stop talking.

That's not overthinking. That's strategy.

And the people around you will feel the difference before they can see it. Meetings will run differently. Decisions will happen faster. Stakeholders will start coming to you—because you're the one who brings clarity.

That's the shift.

Derek saw it in me years before I could see it in myself.

John made it happen in 90 days.

Joshua proved it could happen in 90 seconds.

Now it's your turn.

IT STARTS WITH ONE

Chapter 9 ended with a promise.

One person with these skills is powerful. An entire team? Unstoppable.

I didn't write this book for fun. I wrote it because I got tired of watching the same thing play out across different companies, industries, and roles—often without anyone even realizing it was happening.

It's not something anyone notices immediately.

Nothing changed on the calendar. Same recurring meeting. Same invitees. Everyone ready for the weekly 45-minute update.

Except this time, you change your approach.

Instead of hopping right into the slides, going through each bullet point, you pause.

"Before we jump in—let's confirm what decision we're here to make?"

Not to derail the meeting. Not to sound clever.

You know that if no one can answer that, the meeting is a waste of time.

The room pauses.

Everyone looks up from their phones and laptops.

Someone finally clears their throat and blurts it out: "I don't think we've confirmed that yet."

Perfect. Now we're getting somewhere.

So instead of presenting your slides, you clarify priorities. Surface assumptions. The conversation shifts from explaining to deciding.

The meeting ends a bit early.

Not because it failed.

Because it worked.

One of the attendees stops you in the hallway: "That was the most productive meeting we've had in months. Kudos."

You smile because you know.

She wasn't the only one. Everyone knows.

But here's where it gets good.

There was someone else in that room.

Nadina. A senior analyst. Quiet. Always prepared. Rarely heard.

She watched as you put aside the deck and asked the question. She was surprised to see how quickly the room shifted.

That day, for the first time, she chimed in.

She didn't say much—just one line: "I actually pulled some data on that last week. I think I can answer part of that question."

Everyone in the room turned to her, stunned she wanted to take the lead. The VP said, "Go ahead."

Nadina shared what she'd found—clear, concise, relevant.

The VP nodded slowly. Then he said, "That makes sense. Let's get everyone on board. Can you lead the next deep dive?"

Nadina looked up—caught off guard.

In the last two years of being at the company, nobody had ever asked her to lead anything. They'd asked her to pull data. To update a report. To send the deck. To fix the formatting. To add one more chart.

Not lead.

It happened because the room was now in a different mode.

You changed the energy. She stepped into it.

The next week, Nadina tried it herself—on her own stakeholder call. Different room. Different team. Same question.

She opened with the decision. Skipped the long slide deck. Focused on the three things her manager had been complaining about for months.

Someone in the team leaned forward and asked, "How do we move forward with this?"

The words she needed to hear.

Nadina got approval on the first pass—the first time in two years.

She sat in her car for ten minutes before driving home, still replaying what happened in the meeting—how fast she got approval, how on board the team was.

She knew that things had changed. She was no longer the order-taker.

She's all in.

Now there are two of you.

Then two becomes four.

Four becomes a team.

I've watched this happen at large oil companies. At a government agency in DC. At a mid-size healthcare company in Chicago. At a fintech startup where the whole data team was under 30 and convinced that better models were the answer to everything.

The result is the same.

Meetings get shorter—not because leadership mandated it, but because people stop showing up with 30 slides and start showing up with one clear story, one clear decision to be made.

Stakeholders stop asking for "more data" because someone finally created alignment with the storyboard before building anything.

That one question saves weeks of wasted work.

Dashboards start actually getting used. Not the six-percent log-in-and-bounce kind. The kind where your director checks them before walking into her staff meeting. The kind where someone in finance sends you a message saying, "This is the first dashboard I've actually used more than twice."

Your director notices that ad hoc requests have dropped. Adoption has climbed. Decisions are being made. Projects that used to take three rounds of approval start getting greenlit in one.

Nobody can quite explain what changed.

But you can.

And here's what's amazing.

Once you understand how people actually make decisions, everything changes. Every meeting. Every conversation. Every negotiation. Every interaction with your kids, your partner, your friends.

You start noticing when people are ready. When they're resisting. When they've already decided but haven't said it yet. When they need one more thing before they can commit.

This was never just about dashboards or slide decks.

It's about humans.

How we process.

How we decide.

How we move from "that's interesting" to "let's do this."

You have a system for it now.

YOUR EDGE IN THE AI AGE

Let's talk about AI. Because if you're not paying attention, you're already behind.

AI is coming for your tasks—the technical work, the admin work. It already has.

Dashboards that used to take weeks? AI builds them in minutes.

SQL queries, data cleaning, exploratory analysis—all automated.

The reports you spent your weekend perfecting? A machine can draft and format them in minutes with a single prompt.

If your entire value is "I build things with data," you're a dinosaur. AI builds things with data faster, cheaper, and without complaining about the requirements.

AI can even read rooms—sentiment analysis, facial recognition, engagement detection on video calls. There are tools right now that can flag when an audience is losing interest. And they'll only get more accurate.

So, if your edge is "I can read body language and AI can't"—that edge also has an expiration date.

But here's what won't expire.

People don't buy in to machines—at least not yet. They buy in to people.

Even if AI could read every signal in the room perfectly—detect every nod, every crossed arm, every pronoun shift—it still can't do the thing that actually drives a decision.

It can't be the human in the room that a VP trusts enough to commit $2 million.

It can't sit across from a CFO and say, "I think we're avoiding the real question here," and have that land because of a relationship built over years.

It can't choose to be vulnerable in a presentation. It can't share the story that makes a skeptical executive think, "She gets it. She understands what we're up against."

Sure, it can build trust. But not the kind that makes a CFO say yes. The kind that forms when someone believes you understand the stakes, the politics, and the consequences they'll personally carry if a decision goes wrong.

And without relational trust, there is no buy-in. Antonio Damasio proved that decisions are emotional before they're logical. And emotional commitment flows between humans, not between a human and an algorithm.

The Buy-In Method is the system that gives you the edge—not because it competes with AI, but because it does the one thing AI makes even more important: it helps you be the human that other humans trust enough to act.

The more data AI generates, the more someone needs to stand in front of a room and make it matter.

That someone is you.

Not because you're the smartest person in the room, but because you're the one they trust to move the room.

That's not a skill that gets automated.

That's the skill that makes you irreplaceable.

THE BUY-IN METHOD MANIFESTO

Every movement begins with beliefs.

Not slogans. Not laminated value statements. Not culture decks that sound inspiring on a careers page and disappear the moment a real decision must be made.

Beliefs are different. They're convictions—the kind that hold when the market shifts, when the tools change, when the buzzwords rotate, and when the pressure is real. They don't bend based on who's in the room or how senior the audience is. They define how you show up.

I've been refining these beliefs for over a decade.

Every workshop. Every keynote. Every meeting. Every conversation with a data team who did everything right—and still struggled to get any form of adoption or action.

These beliefs are the foundation of everything I teach. And everything you've learned in this book.

They're mine. But if you've made it this far, I suspect they're becoming yours too.

We can't keep working this way.

We can't keep pushing data and hoping something sticks.

We can't keep sharing insights and hoping they magically turn into action.

We can't keep giving great presentations that go nowhere.

We can't keep being evaluated on outcomes we had no influence over.

This manifesto is where we draw the line in the sand.

1. 88% of insights never influence a single decision. We're here to change that. Tools weren't the problem. Data wasn't the problem. The problem is the gap between insight and action. We're the ones finally closing it.
2. Decisions are made with emotions, not data. Data informs logic. Emotions trigger action. We work with human nature, not against it.
3. We are partners, not order-takers. We don't sit in the corner waiting for the next request. We create clarity from the first question to the final decision.
4. We don't push and pray—we measure buy-in in real time. Hope is not a strategy. We watch for the Three Signs: Clarity, Buy-In, Action. If we see resistance, we adjust. If we see momentum, we accelerate.
5. If it doesn't build decision readiness, it doesn't matter. Our meetings, our analysis, our storyboards—everything we do exists to help leaders make better, faster decisions.

6. Insights only matter when they drive action. Pretty dashboards mean nothing. Brilliant analysis means nothing. If nothing happens after your presentation, it wasn't influence. It was information.
7. We're closing the gap between insights and action. One room. One meeting at a time. This is the shift the industry has been waiting for.

That's what we believe. Now it's time to claim who you are.

The Buy-In Method isn't just a framework.

It's a way of working, a new way of thinking, a new way of communicating, and a way of influencing.

It's the skill set we never knew we needed but now can't live without. It's the movement that changes everything. And it starts with you.

The Oath

I want you to do something.

Read this out loud.

Don't just skim it.

Your voice activates something in your brain that reading silently doesn't. Researchers at the University of Waterloo call it the "production effect"—the dual action of speaking and hearing yourself creates a deeper, more personal imprint than silent reading ever could. And as Damasio proved, decisions are emotional before they're logical. When you hear yourself say these words, you're not just reading a page. You're making a commitment.

Stand up if you can.

Close the door if you need to.

And say this like you mean it.

Because this isn't a motivational exercise. This is you drawing a line.

Between who you were before this book and who you are now.

Here's the oath:

I create clarity, not noise.

I measure buy-in, not just user adoption.

I drive action, not analysis paralysis.

I build decision readiness, not resistance.

I am a decision driver.

And this is how we change the industry.

Screenshot that. Post it. Tag me. I want to see it.

Because every time one more person says those words out loud, the movement gets stronger. Every time someone posts that oath and a colleague asks, "What's a decision driver?"—that's the ripple. That's how it spreads.

One voice at a time.

THE VISION

Right now, most organizations don't have a decision problem. They have an influence problem.

Look around. You'll see it everywhere:

Brilliant analysts turned chart monkeys. Dashboards that impress but get ignored.

Data scientists whose work never sees the light of day—buried in spreadsheets, lost in silos.

Managers drowning in data, starving for clarity.

Leaders flooded with insights, unsure what to act on.

This isn't a skills problem. This isn't a tooling problem.

This is an influence problem.

And influence problems don't get fixed by upgrading technology. They get fixed when organizations realize the bottleneck isn't information readiness—it's decision readiness.

Because insights alone don't create value. Decisions do.

Revolutions don't happen overnight. But they do happen.

Here's what the next three years look like when even a small group adopts the Buy-In Method.

Year 1: The First Movers

A handful of people stop pushing reports and hoping for action. They start creating clarity, measuring buy-in, and driving action. Momentum builds quietly. Leaders notice. Projects succeed. Decisions accelerate. Whispered conversations start: "Whatever they're doing. . . it works." Leaders lean forward. Nod. Small wins compound. One person at a time.

Year 2: The Ripple Effect

Teams pick it up. Meetings stop dragging along. Roadmaps stop stalling. Leaders stop saying: "I'm not seeing what you're seeing." Decision drivers emerge—promoted not for tenure, not for title, but for impact. Clarity spreads. Teams talk in a shared language: "Clarity nods, buy-in questions. No need for another session before the final presentation." The culture begins to shift—slowly, quietly, one person at a time.

Year 3: The New Standard

The industry catches on. Decision readiness becomes the new currency. Conferences teach it. Teams hire for it. Executives demand it. Insight alone no longer impresses. Actionable influence does. Decision drivers become the new class of professionals shaping the future of data. Organizations finally close the gap between insight generated and action taken. The $777 billion crisis starts shrinking.

This is where you step in.
Not to follow. To lead.
You won't wait for permission.
You won't wait for luck.
You'll turn insights into action.
You'll inspire others to do the same.

Because the future isn't about data alone. It's about the people who make data matter.

YOUR MOVE

I started this journey because I had no choice.

I couldn't hope my way to influence. I had to build a system.

It cost me years—failed presentations, pretty dashboards that no one used, nights in hotel rooms staring at the ceiling wondering what I was doing wrong.

But it also changed my life.

Every framework in this book was born from a failure.

The discovery questions came from building the wrong thing for six weeks because I never asked what the stakeholder actually needed.

The storyboard method came from watching a VP snap a screenshot of a whiteboard and say, "Finally, we're on the same page!"

The Three Signs came from Derek telling me to stop talking and start watching.

None of this was theory. All of it was from real world experience.

And now that system is yours.

But tools don't change careers. Decisions do.

You can read ten books on influence and never influence anyone.

You can attend every workshop and still walk into your next meeting hoping it goes well.

The difference between the person who read this book and the person who became a decision driver?

Action.

So here's what I'm asking you.

Use it. This week. Not next month.

Not "when the timing is right."

Not after you've reviewed your notes one more time. This week.

Here's your first assignment.

And yes, I'm giving you homework in a manifesto chapter.

Because manifestos without action are just motivational posters.

Monday morning, walk into your next meeting and ask the decision question before you show a single slide "What decision is this meeting meant to support?"

Watch what happens to the room. Watch who leans forward. Watch who finally says what everyone was thinking.

That same week, take your current project. Before you build one more chart or add one more metric, write a one-page storyboard.

What's the decision?

What's the story?

What's the one thing that matters?

Show it to your stakeholders before you build anything.

Within 30 days, present your next recommendation and watch for the signs.

The nods—are they slow and deliberate or fast and empty?

The questions—are they clarifying or challenging?

The language—do they say "your project" or "our project"?

That's influence, happening in real time.

And when it works—and it will—don't keep it to yourself. Show someone else.

Be the Nadina on someone else's team.

Be the person who changes the room just by changing how you show up.

That's how movements start. Not with a conference. Not with a mandate. With one person doing something different and someone else asking, "What was that?"

Everything you need to keep going is at drivingbuyin.com.

The planning canvas.

The Three Signs checklist.

The discovery question templates.

Video walkthroughs of every framework.

And a growing community of decision drivers who are done hoping their work gets noticed and have decided to make sure it does.

Join the community.

Share your wins.

Post the moment you get your first real-time buy-in read.

Tell us about the meeting that went differently.

Share the Slack message from the colleague who tried your question and got approval for the first time.

The method works. But the community is what makes it stick. When you're surrounded by people who think the same way—who measure instead of hope, who read rooms instead of pray—the whole game changes. You stop feeling like the only one. Because you're not.

You're not alone in this. You never were.

This book is not about data. Not about dashboards.

It's about you. Standing in a room. Knowing that what you do matters.

And having the skill to make sure everyone else knows it too.

It's about every data professional who has ever walked out of a meeting thinking, "They didn't get it," and wondering if the problem was them or the data.

It's neither.

It was always the influence.

And now you have a system for it.

You're not just presenting data anymore.

You're driving decisions.

You're reading rooms.

You're measuring influence in real time.

You're a decision driver.

And the world needs more of us.

There are millions of data professionals out there right now—brilliant people doing incredible work.

And 88% of their insights will never drive a single decision.

Not because the work isn't good enough, but because nobody taught them how to land it.

You can change that. One meeting at a time. One team at a time. One industry at a time.

It starts with one.

It started with me in California.

It started with you in Chapter 1.

Post your Oath. Tag #DecisionDriver. That's how we find each other.

Now go do what you were built to do.

I'll see you in the community.

Let's drive buy-in!

ACKNOWLEDGMENTS

Twelve years. Fortune 500 boardrooms. Stages around the world. A podcast that grew into a cult following. And somehow... here we are. A whole book.

I didn't do this alone.

To God—for an unbelievable career I never could have imagined. Far beyond belief. Baruch Hashem.

To my dear mother Nadina—your strength, intelligence, diligence, and prayers built the foundation I stand on today. You dressed me for success and were behind the scenes before anyone knew my name. Everything I've become started with your sacrifices and love.

To my sister Soo Tang Yuk—my best friend, cofounder, and operator. You created the Mico Yuk brand. You believed in this mission when it cost you to believe. I couldn't have done this without you.

To Anna Maria—my little sister, who poured years into this company as my designer. You make everything I create look better than I imagined.

To my aunt Tamica—for holding down the office in the early days.

To Cabria and Joshua—my niece and great-nephew, my inspiration.

To my best friend Melissa—for your support and never-ending prayers.

To Dean Temares—you pushed me out of an MBA and into finding what I really loved. Best advice I ever received.

ACKNOWLEDGMENTS

To Rick and Cliff—your mentorship led me to many discoveries in this book.

To Ollie Hughes—from our Count days, for your ongoing support and feedback.

To Ryan—my sounding board for every crazy idea and 11 p.m. voice note.

To Barnes & Noble at Perimeter—I practically lived on your floor, pulling every data visualization book off the shelf. That's where the first methodology was born. I came back to write part of this book there too. Fun times.

To the late Ron Reago and Sebastian Walczynski—the first to invest in our methodology. Once you believed, everyone else followed. Ron, I wish you were here to see this.

To Bjorn Johansson—you pressure-tested every idea. Every tough question made this framework stronger.

To the organizations that took a chance on us—Shell, Kimberly-Clark, Nestlé, Ericsson, Qatargas, and more. You let us prove that this works.

To the stages that gave me a voice—Google, Meta, SAP Insider, Microsoft Power BI Community, and organizations worldwide. Every keynote sharpened these ideas.

To my 20,000+ students—your breakthroughs became my case studies. Your struggles shaped my teaching. This book is yours as much as mine.

To the Wiley team—James Minatel, Christine O'Connor, John Sleeva, and the entire crew who turned my voice into something publishable without killing what made it mine. Thank you for protecting the fire.

To the Caribbean island of Montserrat—where my 5K runs to the beach gave me headspace to write. Cherise, thank you for sharing your conference room with me to write. John Osborne, thank you for reigniting my passion for AI. Your curiosity and drive are contagious.

And finally, to every data professional who's ever felt invisible in a room full of executives—thank you!

This book is for you.

Let's get to work.

—Mico Yuk

ABOUT THE AUTHOR

Mico Yuk is a data storyteller, keynote speaker, and creator of the BI Data Storytelling Framework and The Buy-In Method—which teach professionals how to turn insights into action and measure stakeholder influence in real time.

For over a decade, Yuk has trained more than 20,000 data professionals at Fortune 500 companies, including JPMorgan, IBM, Microsoft, Amazon, and Zoom, and has delivered keynotes on stages in over 30 countries. She previously founded and led her own SAP consulting firm.

A former data scientist turned stakeholder influence expert, Yuk combines behavioral science with data expertise to help professionals move from order-takers to decision drivers.

Yuk hosted the award-winning *Analytics on Fire* podcast, is a LinkedIn Learning instructor, former Microsoft MVP and Regional Director, and has appeared as a data commentator on CNN and MSNBC. She is the author of Data Visualization for Dummies (Wiley) and *Driving Buy-In* is her latest book.

Born in the Caribbean, she now splits her time between Atlanta and the islands she calls home.

INDEX

Numerics

4Ds mirror, 20
4-tile structure, 119–127
    Goal Banner, 120–121
    One-Screen Rule, 124–125
    from storyboard to slide deck, 125–127
    Three Decision Tiles, 121–124
90-day path, 167–171
90-day system, 20–22, 178
    weeks 1–4: discovery, 178–179
    weeks 5–8: storyboarding, 179
    weeks 9–12: three signs, 180
90-day truth, 177–178
$777-billion breakdown, 1–12

A

"accelerate decisions", 2
acceleration crisis, decision, 2–4
    missing skills, 3–4
    wrong tools, 3
action, timeline test, 57–59
AI age, 192–193
Angelou, Maya, 143
art of storyboarding, 90–91
The Ask Method, 66

B

Beane, Billy, 48–50
Berger, Thomas, 63
Blueprint, KPI (key performance indicator), 16
BLUF. *See* Bottom Line Up Front (BLUF)
Bottom Line Up Front (BLUF), 117
buy-in
    present to win, 149–150
    questions test, 55–57
buy-in measurement, 20–22
    action (timeline thinking), 23–24
    buy-in (the questions), 23
    clarity (the Nod), 22–23
buy-in method, 24–26, 31, 49
    manifesto, 193–195

INDEX

C

Cabria, 175–177
Churchill, Winston, 117–118
Cialdini, Robert, 58
clarity, nod test, 54–55
The Closing, 156–158
    design close, 158
    discovery close, 157
    status update close, 158
    storyboard close, 157
cover your butt (CYA), 3
Cowan, Nelson, 87
crippling impostor syndrome, 6

D

Damasio, Antonio, 9, 11, 48
data consulting, 2
Data Storytelling (4D) Framework™, 25, 27, 36–38
    define: create stories that stick, 39–41
    deliver: present to win, 42–43
    design: create visuals that drive action, 41–42
    discover: ask the right questions, 38–39
data storytelling storyboard, 91–93
data teams, 6
data tool budgets, 2
data visualization, 7
DBP. *See* death by PowerPoint (DBP)
dead on arrival (DOA), 2, 10, 32
death by PowerPoint (DBP), 10

decision
    acceleration crisis, 2–4
    drivers, 60–62
    as emotional, 9–12
decision-makers, 7, 137
Decision Tile
    anatomy of, 116–118
    build the first, 136–137
    build the second and third, 137–138
    delivery formula: stay in human mode, 153–154
    adjust based on what you see, 155–156
    ask yourself a question about them, 155
    pause, 154
    say the content, 154
    watch for the three signs of influence, 155
design close, 158
design visuals, drive action, 118–119
discover: ask the right questions, 38–39, 63–84
    need context first, 67–68
    questions in action, 74–75
    questions work, 75–80
    reveal readiness, 69–73
discovery close, 157
Discovery #1—Story, 14–20
Discovery #2—Signals, 15
Drucker, Peter, 13, 45
dual-channel questions, 65, 67, 74, 78, 79

INDEX

E
"educated decision", 11
emotional, decisions as, 9–12
emotional intelligence (EQ), 6
engagement, rules of, 95

F
Ford, Henry, 66

G
GDPs, 2
Goal Banner, 120–121, 135
Groundhog Day, 91
"gut decision", 2

H
Huang, Karen, 23

I
imagery (visual) channel, 66, 76, 77
influence, signs of, 22, 24–26, 45–47, 53, 59–60
   action, timeline test, 57–59
   buy-in, questions test, 55–57
   clarity, nod test, 54–55
insights-to-decision breakdown, 4

J
Jennifer, 74

K
kill buy-in, 31–33
   The Gap, 32

The Gut, 31–32
The Myth, 32
KPI (key performance indicator), 87
   Blueprint, 16, 17

L
Levesque, Ryan, 66
Lewis, John, 147

M
metric formula, 17
metric owner, 17
Mico's approach, 87
Miller, George, 87
missing piece, 43–44
movement, 185–187
   actual changes, 187–188
   starts with one, 188–191

N
Nadina, 171–174
nod test, 54–55

O
One-Screen Rule, 124–125
order-taker mode, 81
overthinker mode, 81

P
"people problem", 4–6, 48–51
problem-solver mode, 81
proof of concept (POC), 64
Push-and-Hope method, 33–34

INDEX

Q
"Q3 Revenue Metrics", 125
questions test, buy-in, 55–57

R
real alignment crisis, 88–90
Rukeyser, Muriel, 27

S
Schultz, Howard, 19
Schumacher, E. F., 113
self-sabotage, 180–181
sequence matters, 59–60
Shaw, George Bernard, 85
Simon, Herbert A., 1
SMEs. *See* subject matter experts (SMEs)
Stark, Tony, 35
status update close, 158
Stepford Wives, 55
storyboard
  close, 157
  contract, 107
  data storytelling, 91–93
  when to use the storyboard (and when to skip it), 109–111
  works, 108–109
storyboarding, art of, 90–91
storyboard sprints
  align the vision (60–90 minutes), 93–100
    actions (15–20 minutes), 99
    goal (20–25 minutes), 96–97
    how to run the sprint, 96–99
    insights (15–20 minutes), 98–99
    key metrics (20–25 minutes), 97–98
    rules of engagement, 95
    setup, 95
  commit to action (60 minutes), 104–108
    data disagrees, 105
    lock in the commitment, 106–107
    walking back into the room, 104–105
    walkthrough, 105–106
    what you leave with, 107–108
  validate the plan (24–48 hours), 100–104
    mindset, 103–104
    process, 101–102
    updated storyboard, 103
    validation checklist, 102–103
    what to watch for, 101
subject matter experts (SMEs), 94
"surrogation trap", 88

T
timeline test, action, 57–59
touchpoints, death by a thousand, 145–147
transformation, 181–182

V
verbal (logic) channel, 66, 76, 77
vision, 196–198

W

"what's in it for me (WIIFM)", 59

Win Trust in 60 Seconds, 150–153
   set expectations (30 seconds), 152–153
   show why it matters (20 seconds), 152
   start with a short greeting, 151–152

Z

zero incentive, 3